Hymn to Kali

Karpuradi-Stotra –

To the Hindu Goddess, Incarnation of Parvati and Wife to Shiva

By Sir John Tyler Woodroffe

(AKA Arthur Avalon)

PANTIANOS CLASSICS

Published by Pantianos Classics

ISBN-13: 978-1-78987-139-5

First published in 1922

Contents

Publisher's Note ..... *v*

Preface ..... *vi*

Invocation ..... *xv*

Hymn to Kālī 32

Verse One 32

Verse Two 35

Verse Three 37

Verse Four 40

Verse Five 42

Verse Six 44

Verse Seven 46

Verse Eight 48

Verse Nine 50

Verse Ten 51

Verse Eleven 53

Verse Twelve 55

Verse Thirteen 56

Verse Fourteen 57

Verse Fifteen 59

Verse Sixteen 61

Verse Seventeen 63
Verse Eighteen 65
Verse Nineteen 67
Verse Twenty 69
Verse Twenty-One 70
Verse Twenty-Two 71

Publisher's Note

The Orientalists' system of transliteration has followed in this work.

अ a, आ ā, इ i, ई ī, उ u, ऊ ū, ऋ ṛ, ॠ ṝ, ऌ ḷ, ॡ ḹ
ए e, ऐ ai, ओ o, औ au, ं ṃ or ṁ, : ḥ.

क् k, ख् kh, ग् g, घ् gh, ङ् ṅ,

च् c, छ् ch, ज् j, झ् jh, ञ् ñ,

ट् ṭ, ठ् ṭh, ड् ḍ, ढ् ḍh, ण् ṇ,

त् t, थ् th, द् d, ध् dh, न् n,

प् p, फ् ph, ब् b, भ् bh, म् m,

य् y, र् r, ल् l, व् v, श् s',

ष् ṣ, स् s, ह् h, ळ् ḷ.

Preface

THIS celebrated Kaula *Stotra*, which is now translated from the Sanskrit for the first time, is attributed to Mahākāla Himself. The Text used is that of the edition published at Calcutta in 1899 by the Sanskrit Press Depository, with a commentary in Sanskrit by the late Mahāmahopādhyāya Kṛṣhṇanātha Nyāya-pañcānana, who was both very learned in Tantra-Śāstra and faithful to his Dharma. He thus refused the offer of a good Government Post made to him personally by a former Lieutenant-Governor on the ground that he would not accept money for imparting knowledge.

Some variants in reading are supplied by this commentator. I am indebted to him for the Notes, or substance of the notes, marked K. B. To these I have added others, both in English and Sanskrit explaining matters and allusions familiar doubtless to those for whom the original was designed, but not so to the English or even ordinary Indian reader. I have also referred to the edition of the *Stotra* published by Gaṇeśa-Candra-Ghoṣa at Calcutta in 1891, with a translation in Bengali by Gurunātha Vidyānidhi, and commentary by Durgārāma-Siddhāntavāgīśa Bhattācārya. I publish for the first time Vimalānanda-Svāmī's Commentary to which I again refer later. When in this Introduction or in the Commentary I have not mentioned these two works my authorities are the Tantras or Tāntrik works which I cite, or. the information I have gathered from those whom I have consulted.

One of the chief features of this *Stotra* is that it gives the *mantroddhāra* of the Dakshina-Kālikā. It not only gives us the *Dhyāna*, *Yantra*, *Sādhana* and *Svarūpa-varnanā* of the Mahādevī, but it also contains the chief Mantras of Dakṣiṇakālikā. The adjective "*Tava manu-samuddharaṇajanu*" qualifying "*idam stotram*" in Śloka 21 expressly states this fact.

Among the various Mantras of Dakṣiṇā Kālikā the greatest is the "*Vidyārājñī*" consisting of 22 syllables (*Dvāviṁsākṣarī*). This mantra gives the fullest and the truest symbol of the Svarūpa of Her. This mantra is contained in the first five Ślokas.

The first Śloka contains		*Krīṁ, Krīṁ, Krīṁ*	(3 *akṣaras*)
2nd „	„	*Hūṁ, Hūṁ*	(2 „)
3rd „	„	*Hrīṁ, Hrīṁ*	(2 „)
4th „	„	*Dakṣine Kālike*	(6 „)
5th „	„	*Krīṁ, Krīṁ, Krīṁ, Hūṁ, Hūṁ, Hrīṁ, Krīṁ, Svāhā*	(9 *akṣaras*)

So the first five Ślokas give us altogether 22 *akṣaras i.e.* the full *Vidyārājñī.*

In Vimalānanda-Svāmī's *Tīkā* of the 5th Śloka in the revised Sanskrit text he has proved by quotations from the 9th patala of *Śāktānanda-taranginī* that this 22-syllabled *mantra* is the full and true representation of the Svarūpa of the Mahādevī. See the quotation which begins with

"*Krīm-kāro mastakaṃ devi Krīm-kāraśca lalātakaṁ*"

and ends with

"*Svā-śabdena pada-dvandvam hā-kāreṇa nakhaṁ tathā*"

The words "*Svarūpaṁ*" (5th sl.) and "*Sakalaṁ*" (6th sl.) point to this-*Vidyārājñī.* After the full *Vidyā-rājñī* has been given in the first five Ślokas, the 6th Śloka gives the various other Mantras of less importance and significance—ranging from one syllabled to nine-syllabled, 15-syllabled, 21-syllabled and so forth.

This Mantroddhāra has been made following the authority of Kālikā-śruti, Niruttara-Tantra and other Tantras. Many commentators, however, have apparently in the view of Vimalānanda failed to consult the above authorities, and have thus fallen into errors and have given a different *Mantroddhāra.* Some take the 1st Śloka to give a one-syllabled *mantra,* the 2nd sloka as also the 3rd, two two-syllabled *mantras,* the 5th a nine-syllabled one and so on: a view which it is contended is opposite to such passages as "*atha hainaṁ brahmarandhre brahma-svarūpinīm āpnoti . . . . bṛhad-bhānu-jāyāṁ uccaret*" in the 1st Sūkta of Kālikopaniṣad; or passages in Niruttara-Tantra (Ch. II) beginning with "*Atha vaksye Kuleśāni Dakṣinā-kalikā-manuṁ*" and ending with "*Sarva-mantra-mayī vidyā sṛṣti-sthityanta-kāriṇī.*" The Svāmī further refers me to the end of the Kālikopaniṣad where dealing with the various Mantras of the Dakṣiṇa-Kālikā it is said "*Atha sarvām vidyām prathamaṁ ekaṁ dvayaṁ vā trayaṁ vā nāmatrayaputitaṁ vā kṛtvā japet.*" The great Tāntrik Pūrṇānanda Giri explaining the passage says "*Sarvām vidyām-iti pūrvoktadvāvimśatyakṣaryāh prathama bījaṁ vā bīja-dvayaṁ vā* etc. (vide Śyāmā-rahasyaṁ, Rasikamohan's edition, p. 36.)

From the above consideration, it is clear that at the very beginning in the first 5 Ślokas the 22-syllabled *Mantra* is given and then the others. It may be added here that the fact of Mahākāla's composing the Hymn in 22 Ślokas not more nor less—is also an indication of the correctness of the Svāmī's view, who, in further support of it cites 5 Ślokas dealing with the *Mantroddhāra* from the *Krama-stava* of the Dakṣiṇa-Kālikā under the first 5 Ślokas of the Karpūrādi, which will be found in the printed text.

In course of revising his *Vyākhyā* Vimalānanda-Svāmī has in the first six Ślokas given good grounds to prove that the *Stotra* not only contains the *Mantroddhāra* and the *Sādhana* of Śrī-Śrī-Dakṣina-Kālikā but also in it are given the *Mantras* and *Rahasyapūjā* of Śri-Śri-Tārā and Śrī-Śrī-Tripura-sundarī.

In addition to the Mantroddhāra the following matters are contained in the *Stotra.*

	No. of Slokas
Dhyāna	1, 2, 3, 4, 5, 6, 7, 8, 11
Yantra	18
Sādhana	10, 11, 15, 16, 17, 18, 19, 20
Madya	13
Māṁsa	19
Maithuna	10
Phala-Śruti	21, 22

The Ślokas 9, 12, 14 contain *stuti* only.

Ślokas 10, 15-18, 20 refer to the Tāntrik *vīrācārasādhana*. *Vīrācāra* is for the class of *sādhaka* who are *vīrabhāva* and *abhiṣikta*. To those who follow *paśvācāra* this ritual is strictly forbidden. The nature of the *rahasyapūjā* is indicated in the text, to which I have added an explanatory commentary in English and Sanskrit.

To the *Paśu*, *sādhana* by night is prohibited, for it connotes in Śākta-sādhana, worship with the *Pañcatattva*. The *Paśu* is still bound by the *pāśa* (bonds) of desire, etc., and he is, therefore, not *adhikārī*, for that which, if undertaken by the unfit, will only make these bonds stronger. For him, on the contrary, there are severe restrictions in this matter, for, as the Śāktakrama cited by the commentator says, "*Maithunaṁ tatkathālāpaṁ tadgoṣṭhīṁ parivarjayet.*" (The *Paśu* should avoid *maithuna*, conversation on the subject, and the like.) The *Paśu* should avoid the eight forms of *maithuna* known as *aṣṭāṅga maithuna*—viz., *smaraṇaṁ* (thinking upon it), *kīrtanam* (talking of it), *kelih* (play with women), *prekṣaṇam* (looking upon women), *guhyabhāṣaṇaṁ* (talk in private with women), *saṁkalpah* (wish or resolve for *maithuna*), *adhyavasāyah* (determination towards it), as well as *kriyāniṣpattih* (actual accomplishment). The Nityā Tantra, which the commentator cites, says: "*Rātrau naiva yajed deviṁ sandhyāyāṁ vā'parāhnake*"—"He (the *Paśu* should never worship the Devī during the latter part of the day or in the evening or at night." To this, from amongst many other authorities, I may add the Svatantra, which says that the Paśubhāva Sādhaka should do one lakh of *japa* in day time and that a *Vīra* devoted to his own Ācāra should do one lakh of *japa* at night;

Paśubhāvarato mantrī divā lakṣa japaṁ caret.
Svācāranirato viro rātrau lakṣa japaṁ caret.

In connection with this verse I must observe that in the notes to verse 20 it is said that the first half of the 20th Śloka is meant for "*Paśusādhakas*" and that the 2nd half refers to the "*pūrṇābhiṣiktavīrasādhaka*," as also that the word "*paraṁ*" (afterwards) means and refers to the time when the 'Paśu' having received *abhiṣeka* enters *vīrācāra* and is *adhikārī* for the midnight *puraścaraṇa*. Vimalānanda tells me that this is wrong and that the whole Śloka has reference to the *vīra* or *divya-sādhaka* and that no portion of it refers to the *Paśu-sādhaka*.

The quotation just made from the Svatantra-Tantra no doubt seems to lend support to the view that the first part of the Śloka refers to the Paśu, but he informs me and I fully accept the correction that he and other followers of the Śāstra knew the passage to bear a meaning which is consonant with his view, that is, it means this:—*Mantrī* means the *vīrasādhaka*; the *mantrī* should perform *lakṣa-japa* in the day time following the *ācāra* of the *paśu* (*paśu-bhāvaratah*). The *vīra-sādhaka* should perform *lakṣa-japa* in the night following his own *ācāra* (*svācāra-niratah*). The word "*svācāra*" (own *ācāra*) points to his interpretation being correct.

In support of his view the Svāmī cites the following Verses which all say the same thing namely that the initiate should be Brahmacārī during day and at night worship according to Kulācāra. Kaulāvalī says:

Naktaṁ-bhojī haviṣyānnaṁ japed vidyām divā śucih.
Dvivāsāh sarvathā vīro brahmacārī bhavet sadā.
Rātrau saṁpūjayed devīṁ kulācāra-krameṇa tu
Dvijanmanāṁ tu sarveṣam dvidhā vidhi-rihocyate.

Again, Kālikopaniṣad says:

Sāṁbhava-dīkṣāsu ratah śākteṣu vā divā brahmacārī rātrau nagnah sadā maithunāsaktamānasah Japa-pūjādi-niyamaṃ kuryād iti.

Kaulāvalī again says:

Unmukhyāh Kālikāyāśca viśeṣah kathyate 'dhunā.
Divase brahmacaryeṇa sviyasaṁkhyājapaṁ caret.
Rātrau māṁsāsavairmatsyairmudrābhir maithunod-bhavaih.

The reason of the *vīrasādhaka* being instructed to adopt the *ācāra* of *brahmacārī* in the day-time is the necessity for the concealment of the *vīrācāra* from the public which Tantra so often insists upon. Śiva says that *vīrācāra* cannot be understood aright by the common people and therefore must be concealed, as closely as a man should conceal his own mother's sin "*gopayet mātṛ-jāra-vat.*"

Moreover, the worship of Kālī in "*paśvācāra*" is totally forbidden by Śiva. The *Paśu* is precluded by Tantra from the worship of Kālī. For example the Niruttara-Tantra says:

Divya-bhavaṁ vīra-bhāvaṁ vinā Kālīṁ prapūjayet.
Pūjane narakaṁ yāti tasya duhkhaṁ pade pade.
Paśubhāva-rato devi yadi Kālīṁ prapūjayet.
Rauravaṁ narakaṁ yāti yāvad ābhūta-samplavaṁ.

(By the worship of Kālī without *Divyabhāva* and *Vīrabhāva* the worshipper suffers pain at every step and goes to hell. If a man who is of the *Paśubhāva* worships Kālī then he goes to the *Raurava* Hell until the time of final dissolution).

Vimalānanda-Śvāmi says: The worship of Kālī without the use of wine, though seen in many places, is Paurāṇik and not Tāntrik (*i.e.* sanctioned by the Tantra.)

Verses 1-8, 11, the first part of verse 20, and 21 (except at midnight) deal with *japa* of the *mantra* of, and *dhyāna* upon, the Devī, which, of course, may be done by the *Paśu*. Verses 9, 12, 13, and 14 are *stuti*, and 22 is the usual *phala-śloka*, which states the reward to be gained by the reading of the *Stotra*.

Verses 10, 15-18, and the second portion of verse 20 deal with *Latāsādhana*. The *śakti* of this *sādhana* is ordinarily the own wife of the *sādhaka*, married according to the Vaidik injunctions; the *svaśakti* or *ādyāśaktī*, as she is technically called in Tantra. One's own wife is Ādyā-Śaktī and *Sādhana* should be done with her aid (*Ādyā-śaktīh svadārāh syāt tāmevaśṛtya sādhayet*). With her is practised that *śaktīsādhana*, the aim of which is the acquirement of self-control, which, checking the outward-going current, places the *sādhaka* upon the path of *nivṛtti*. Indeed, the Kaulikārcanadīpikā says, "Without *ādyā śakti* worship is but evil magic". (*Ādyāśaktiṁ vinā pūjā abhicārāya kalpate*). It is only the *siddha*, which term is here used in the special sense of one who has obtained complete control over his passions, to whom is permitted another *śakti* (*paraśakti*). So the Prāṇatoṣinī quotes, "a man shall obtain *siddhi* with his own *śakti*, and afterwards (that is, when he is *siddha*) he should make *japa* with *paraśakti*" (*Svaśaktau siddhim āpnuyāt paraśaktau tadā japet*). And similarly Niruttara Tantra says, that the *sādhaka* who is *siddha* in Kulācāra may worship "another" woman. (*Siddhamantrī kulācāre parayoṣām prapūjayet*). In both these cases *paraśakti* has a double meaning viz., "another" woman that is corporeal woman, or "Supreme" that is the Supreme Woman who in the body is Kuṇḍalinī-Śakti. This latter appears to be sense in the quotation which speaks of the *siddhamantrī*. It has been said also, as in the Mahānirvāṇa Tantra, that *paraśakti* must (if unmarried) be married either by Vaidika or Śaiva rites, or (if married and the husband is dead) according to the latter rite. Further, that which determines the moral character of an act is the intention with which it is done. As the Kaulāvalīya says, when a man's intention is bad then his act is so, otherwise there is no fault:

Ata eva yadā yasya vāsanā kutsitā bhavet.
Tadā doṣāya bhavati nānyathā dūṣaṇaṁ kvacit.

As an example of the same act and varying intention, it is aptly said: "A wife is kissed with one feeling and a daughter's face with another". (*Bhāvena cumbitā kāntā bhāvena duhitrānanam*). A *Mantrin* who is given over to lust, for the subjugation of which the *sādhana* is prescribed, goes, as is said in the Tantrasāra, to the Hell called Raurava. (*Lingayonirato mantrī raurakang narakang brajet*). In the words of the Āhārabheda-Tantra—*Vāmācāro bhavet tatra vāmā bhūtvā yajet parām*. "One may be a Vāmācārī if one can worship *Vāmā* being oneself a woman." This is on the principle that a worshipper should always be like the object of his worship. Woman is *Devatā*, and the embodiment of the Supreme Śakti, and is as such honoured and worshipped, and is, when *pūjyā śakti*, never the subject of enjoyment.

Verses 15 and 16, as sufficiently appears from their context, refer to the *sādhana* of those who are not *siddha*.

Verses 10, 17, and 18 apply to both *sādhaka* and *siddha*, as to verse 20, see *ante*.

By such *sādhana* the last vestiges of the most powerful of such bonds is sought to be destroyed, and with such destruction the seed of *karma* and rebirth. He, like Śiva, becomes destroyer of Smara, and Śiva Himself. Verses 4, 18, and 20 refer directly to this fruit of sādhana. Others indicate the material and intellectual greatness on earth of the sādhaka, who devoutly worships the Devī. To him is given mastery over all persons and things of the world, which on death, if siddha, he leaves for the dwelling by the Supreme Feet (verse 17), or Nirvāṇa. As Śiva says in the Kālīvilāsa-Tantra "I have told you, my beloved, all about the five Tattvas, Sādhana in the cremation ground and with the funeral pyre now listen to the doctrine of the Siddha-vīra."

Madyaṁ matsyaṁ tathā māṁsaṁ mudrāṁ maithunam-eva ca.
Śmaśānasādhanaṁ bhadre citāsādhanam eva ca.
Etat to kathitaṁ sarvaṁ siddhaviramataṁ śṛiṇu.

It is the *sādhana* of the cremation-ground on which all passion is burnt away. There are two kinds of cremation-ground, of which the one is the funeral pyre (*citā*), and the other *yonirūpā mahākālī*. As the first Chapter of the Niruttara-Tantra says there are two cremation grounds namely that which is the funeral pyre and the *yoni* which, in its *sūkṣma* sense, is the Devī, the *śmasāna* being in the same sense dissolution or *pralaya*. (*Śmaśānam dvividhaṁ devi chitā yoni prakīrtitā*). In even the *sthūla* sense the *sādhaka* must be *susādhaka*, for union without right disposition—*japa, dhyāna* etc.—is the animal *maithuna* of a *paśu*.

Śloka 19 refers to animal and human sacrifice to Kālī. Reference to this sacrifice is also made in the Kālikā-Purāṇa, and the Tantrasāra speaks of a substitute in the figure of a man made of the paste of cereals. The latter work also says that by the sacrifice of a man one acquires great prosperity, and the eight *siddhis*. (*Naradatte maharddhih syād aṣtasiddhir-anuttamā*). But it adds that this is not for all. For the Brāhmaṇa may not make such a sacrifice. (*Brāhmaṇānāṁ narabalidāne nādhikārah*). And if he does so, he goes to Hell. Moreover according to K. B., who cites as his authority the Yāmala quoted in the Kālīkalpalatā, the King alone can make such a sacrifice.

This leads one to point out that the Hymn has other than these gross (*Sthūla*) meanings. In Brāhamanism everything has three aspects—Supreme (*Para*), Subtle (*Sūkṣma*) and Gross (*Sthūla*). Thus the nineteenth Śloka when referring to the sacrifice of various animals and of man himself intends according to the subtle sense the six great sins for which they stand, ranging from Lust (goat) to Pride (man). It is these which must be sacrificed by the knowers who are worshippers of the Mother the age of material sacrifice, so universal throughout the world, having passed away. So again the word Paraśakti may refer to the Supreme Śakti or may be used in the sense of a Śakti other than the *svaśakti* or Sādhaka's wife who, may in the case of the competent (*adhikārī*) be an associate in the worship on the principle stated in the Guhyakālīkhaṇda of the Mahākāla-Saṁhitā.

"As is the competency of the Sādhaka, so must be that of the Sādhikā. In this way only is success attained and not otherwise even in ten million years".

Yādṛśah sādhakah proktah Sādhikā'pi ca tādṛśah
Tatah siddhim-avāpnoti nānyathā varṣa-kotibhih.

This principle rests on the fact that man and woman together make one whole and can only co-operate in the rites where the attainments or *Adhikāra* of each is the same. But this does not necessarily mean that such co-operation is by *Maithuna* in its sexual sense; quite the contrary. In the same way in the Vaidik ritual the wife is *Sahadharmiṇī*. But such ritual is only for the competent within the bounds of Śāstric injunction for, as the Śaktisaṇgama Tantra (Part IV) says,—"Though a man be a knower of the three times, past, present and future and though he be a controller of the three worlds, even then he should not transgress the rules of conduct for men in the world were it only in his mind".

Yadyapyasti trikālajñas-trailokyāvarṣaṇakṣamāh.
Tathā'pi laukikācāram manasā'pi na laṅghayet.

But *Paraśakti* again may mean no woman at all, but Supreme Śakti or the Mother Herself whose forms they are and in such sense the union of the Sādhaka is with the "woman" within himself—the Kuṇdalinī Śakti who in Yoga unites with Her Supreme Husband Paramaśiva. (See A. Avalon's "Serpent Power"). The context must be known as in the misunderstood saying "*Maithunena mahāyogī mama tulyo na saṁśayah,*" which does not mean, as a recent English work on Hinduism suggests, that by sexual connection (*Maithuna*) the *Mahāyogī* becomes without doubt the equal of Śiva or God. This is on its face absurd and had it not been that such criticism is clouded with prejudice the absurdity would be recognised. How can sexual connection make any one God or His equal? The person spoken of is a *Mahāyogī* who, as such, has no connection physical or otherwise with women. *Maithuna* means "action and reaction" and "coupling" and sexual intercourse is only *one form* of such coupling. Thus when Mantra is said there is a coupling or *Maithuna* of the lips. In Yoga there is a coupling (*Maithuna*) of the active and changeless Principles of the Universe. The saying means that the *Mayāyogī* who unites Kuṇḍalī-Śakti in his body with Paramaśiva becomes himself Śiva.

So again it is said in an apparently alarming verse quoted by Tarkālaṁkāra, in his commentary on the Mahānirvāṇa.

Mātṛ-yonau kṣipet liṁgam bhaginyāh-stanamardanaṁ
Guror-mūrdhni padaṁ dattvā punarjanma na vidyate.

This verse in its literal sense means that if any one commits incest with his mother and sister and places his foot on the head of his Guru he is liberated and is never again reborn. But of course that is not the meaning. The first half of the line refers to the placing of the *Jīvātmā* in the triangle situated in the *Mūlādhāra* centre with the *Svayaṁbhuliṅga* in it which triangle is called *Mātṛ-yoni*. The *Liṅga* is the *Jīvātmā*. From this point upwards, after union with Kuṇḍalinī, the *Jīvātmā* is to be led. The union of *jīvātmā* with Kuṇḍalinī is spoken of in the second half of the first line. Kuṇḍalinī is the sister of the *Jīvātmā* both being in the same body. The meaning of the last line is as follows:—after union of Kuṇḍalinī and *Jīvātmā* the united couple are led up to the *Sahasrāra* or thousand-petalled lotus in the head which is situated above the twelve-petalled lotus which again is the abode of the Guru. When the Yogī is above the twelve-petalled lotus his feet may be described as being on the head of the Guru. Moreover it is said that at this point the relationship of Guru and disciple ceases. *Mātṛ-yoni* is also the term given to those sections of the fingers between the joints on which count of the Japa or recital of the mantra is *not* to be done. If *Matṛ-yoniṁ* suggests incest, then this verse is a prohibition of it—*Mātṛ-yoniṁ parityajya viharet sarvayoniṣu*. There are many other technical terms in Tantra-Śāstra which it is advisable to know before criticising it. One of the tests to which an intending disciple may be put consists in being questioned as to such passages. If he is a gross-minded or stupid man his answer will show it.

In order therefore that the Hymn may be understood in its various aspects I have given in the notes explanations of or in respect of its *Sthūla* or gross meaning. This is followed by the valuable commentary given to me, some years ago and now first published, by Vimalānanda-Svāmī which is called *Svarūpavyākhyā*; that is, it gives the subtle (*Sūkṣma*) or, as we should say in English, the inner sense or esoteric meaning according to the teaching of his own Guru Mahāmahopādhyāya-Rāmānandasvāmī-Siddhāntapañcānana. The text books and Commentary are preceded by an admirable little essay of Svāmī Vimalānanda by way of Introduction to the *Vimalānandadāyinī svarūpa-vyakhyā* on his "Lord of Hymns" which is commonly known as the Karpūrādi Stotra chanted by Mahākāla to, and in honour of, Dakṣiṇā-Kālikā. It, as also the inner-sense Commentary are written for those liberation-seeking Sādhakas who, worshipping Śrīvidyā, meditate not on the gross form

(*Sthūlamūrti*) but on the *Svarūpa-tattva* of Brahmavidyā Kālikā. As such many will be glad, as I was, to read it and will derive benefit therefrom.

I may note here that the Svāmī while revising the Vyākhyā, has given a new interpretation of the line "*te Lakṣmī-lāsya-līlā-kamala-dala-dṛśah vāma-rūpāh bhavanti*" in the 5th Śloka and of "*rati-rasa-mahānanda-niratām*" in the 13th Śloka.

On the attainment of *siddhi*, ritual ceases. There is neither sacrifice nor worship, nor *yoga*, *puraścaraṇa*, *vrata*, *japa*, or other *karma*. For all *sādhana* ceases when it has borne its fruit in Siddhi. The Siddha-Kaula is beyond all rules.

For the meaning of these and other terms, the reader is referred to the Author's "Principles of Tantra, (Tantra-tattva)," "Śakti and Śākta," "Serpent-Power" and "Garland of Letters" which is a study on the Mantra-Śāstra; and for other Hymns to the Devī, his and Ellen Avalon's "Hymns to the Goddess," translated from the Sanskrit of the Tantra, Purāṇa, and the Devī-stotra of Śaṁkarācārya, which gives other specimens of the Hindu Hymnal, of which that now published is but one and a special type.

Arthur Avalon
Puri,
30, May 1922.

Invocation

AIM

I make obeisance to the Lord Guru, the wish-granting Tree of Suras, eternal Consciousness and Bliss Itself, the highest of the highest, Brahman, Śiva Himself. I make obeisance to Her who by Her Śakti of three Guṇas creates, maintains, and at the end of the Kalpa withdraws, the world and then alone is. Devoutly I call to mind Her, the Mother of the whole universe, Śivā Herself.

OM

Obeisance to the Supreme Devatā.

Here follows an Introduction to the Vimalānandadāyini Commentary on that Lord of Hymns called the Karpūrādi-Stotra to Śrimad Dakṣiṇa-Kālikā.

All-good and all-powerful Parameśvara is without beginning or end. Though in Himself Nirguṇa He is the Ādhāra of the three Guṇas. Though Himself formless He creates, preserves and withdraws the world of extended matter (Prapañca) by means of the Āvaraṇa and Vikṣepa-Śaktis of His own Māyā which can make that possible which seems impossible. The Śvetāśvatara-Upaniṣad says that by meditation was seen the Sva-śakti of the Deva, who is the abode of all causes, associated with Kālatattva. In the Niruttara-Tantra Śiva speaks of the three-eyed corpse-like One, Nirguṇa but also seat of Guṇas associated with Śakti. Though Himself without beginning, middle or end, He creates and is the material Cause of the world which has a beginning, middle, and end. For this reason the Tantras and other Śāstras call Him Ādinātha, Mahākāla, Paramaśiva and Paramabrahman. It is this unlimited, undivided, beginning-less, and endless Mahākāla who is imagined to be limited by the Sun, Moon and Planets, and, as such, is called by the names of Kalā, Kāṣṭhā, Muhūrta, Yāma, Day, Night, Pakṣa, Month, Season, Half-year, Year, Yuga, Kalpa and so forth. It is He who divides Time into Kāla, Kāṣṭhā and so forth, and as Vyaṣti is called by the name Kalā, and the rest. He is named Paramaśiva Mahākāla when creating, preserving and withdrawing the millions of worlds.

Apart from individual name and form, He exists as the Samaṣti of them and the Endless Supreme Greatness (Paramomahān). Viṣṇu-Purāṇa says that Bhagavān Kāla is without beginning or end. From him appears the limited in creation. Atharvaveda says that Kāla created beings (Prajā) He is Prajāpati. From Kāla was self-born Kaśyapa and Tapas. Mahākāla is omniscient since

He is all pervading, dependent on none, and the Ātmā of ail. Kūrma-Purāṇa also says that he is the Supreme, imperishable, without beginning or end, all-pervading, independent, the Ātmā of all who fascinates (Manohara) all minds by His greatness. Kālamādhava cites Viṣṇu-dharmottara as saying that He is called Kāla because of his dissolving (Kalanāt) all beings, and He is Parameśvara because He is Himself without beginning or end. Mahākala is Himself Nirguṇa and Niṣkriya, but his Śakti makes the Sun and other heavenly lights rise, stay and set.

It is by the Power of the Śakti of Kāla that men and other Jīvas are conceived in the womb, are born, attain childhood, boyhood, middle and old age and leave the world on death. In the Śāntiparva of Mahābhārata, Vedavyāsa says that it is through Kāla that women bear, that birth and death occur, winter, summer and rains come, and the seed germinates. Even Brahmā, Viṣṇu and Rudra appear, stay and disappear through the Śakti of Kāla. None can escape Its operation. Viṣṇu-Saṁhitā says that even those Devas who create and withdraw the world are themselves withdrawn by Kāla. Kāla or time is certainly then the stronger. Mahākāla is called Mahākālī because He is one and the same and not different from His eternal Śakti. It is She who is Mahāvidyā, Mahādevī, Mahāmāyā, and Parabrahmarūpiṇī. As Ādinātha Mahākāla is the first creator of the world so the Śakti of Mahākāla, the merciful Mahākālī is the Ādiguru of the world. Yoginī Tantra says that Mahākālī is the Mother of the world, and one with Mahākāla, as is shown in the Ardhanāriśvara Mūrti.

It was this Brahmavidyā who (Yoginī-Tantra, 10th Patala) at the beginning of this Kalpa was heard as a bodyless voice from the sky by Brahmā, Viṣṇu, and Maheśvara, who were then told to perform Tapasyā for the acquisition of creative and other Śaktis. It was this Aniruddha-saraśvatī who in the Satya-yuga appeared in the Heavens before Indra and other proud Devatās in the form of a brilliant Yakṣa, and crushing the pride of the Devas Agni and Vāyu, in the form of all-beautiful Umā, taught Brahmatattva to Indra, the King of the Devas (See Kenopaniṣad 11, 12).

This Kālī again who is Parameṣtiguru and grants Kaivalya, compassionating the sensuous and short-lived Jīvas of the terrible Kaliyuga revealed the Śāṁbhavī-Vidyā. This, which was taught in the form of conversations between Devī and Īśvara, had been during the three preceding ages kept as concealed as a lady of high family from public gaze. It contained three sets of sixty-four Āgamas each, which revealed the path of Liberation for these Jīvas. Though She is Herself eternal and Saccidānandarūpiṇī, She at times out of compassion for Sādhakas assumes forms fitted for their Sādhanā. Similarly the Veda, Āgama and the rest though everlasting portions of the Śabdabrahmarūpiṇī are only revealed to Sādhakas at different times in the several Yugas.

When the Mahādevī who is Consciousness (Cinmayī) at the beginning of the Kalpa was pleased by the Tapasyā of Deva Rudra, floating on the Causal Waters, She assumed the Virād aspect and became thus visible to Him. At that time by the command of Mahādevī the Deva Rudra saw in the Suṣuṁnā millions of universes (Brahmāṇḍa) and millions of Brahmās, Viṣṇus and Maheśvaras in them. The Deva, greatly wondering in the Heart-Lotus of Mahādevī, there saw the Mūrti of Śabdabrahman consisting of Āgamas, Nigamas, and other Śāstras (See Yoginī-Tantra, 9th Patala). He saw that of that Mūrti, Āgama was the Paramātmā, the four Vedas with their Angas were the Jīvātmā, the six systems of philosophy (Darśana) were the senses, the Mahāpurāṇas and Upapurāṇas were the gross body, the Smṛtis were the hands and other limbs, and all other Śāstras were the hairs of that great Body. He also saw the fifty Mātṛkā (Letters) resplendent with Tejas on the edges and petals of Her Heart-Lotus. Within the pericarp of the Lotus of the Virādrūpiṇī He saw the Āgamas, brilliant as millions of suns and moons, replete with all Dharma and Brahmajñāna, powerful to destroy all Māyā, full of all Siddhis and Brahmanirvāṇa. By the grace of Mahākālī he fully mastered the Veda, Vedānta, Purāṇas, Smṛiti and all other Śāstra. Later, Brahmā and Viṣṇu received this knowledge of Āgama and Nigama from Him.

In the Satyayuga Brahmā revealed the Smṛtis, Purāṇas and other Śāstra to the Devarṣis. In this way Brahmavidyā was promulgated to the world. This therefore is authority to show, that just as Brahman is everlasting, so are the Agamas and Nigamas which tell of Brahman. Just as in the Satya and other Yugas, only the three twice-born castes, wearing the sacred thread, but not the Śūdra and other low castes were entitled to worship according to the Veda, so in those three Yugas only Devarṣis, Brahmarṣis and Rājarṣis, who had conquered their passions and knew Advaita doctrine and Brahman, were entitled to the Āgama Śāstra which destroys all sense of difference caused by ignorance and grants knowledge of Advaitatattva.

By Śiva's command they kept it as secret in their heart as they would a knowledge of their own mother's illicit love. By Upāsanā they became liberated whilst yet living (Jīvanmukta) and attained to Brahmanirvāṇa. At that time the Upāsanā of the Āgama was unknown to Sādhakas devoted to Karma. For this reason many people nowadays think the Tantra-śāstra to be of recent origin. Probably all know that in the first three Yugas Brāhmaṇa boys, after investiture with the sacred thread, used to learn the Karmakāṇda and Jñānakāṇda of the Veda orally from their preceptors. The Veda was not then classified or reduced to writing. Towards the close of the Dvāparayuga, Śrīkṛṣṇa-dvaipāyana Maharṣi Vedavyāsa divided the Veda into four parts and reduced it to writing. This however does not show that the Veda is a recent production. The Supreme Science (Para vidyā) which is contained in the Āgama was also handed down from generation to generation of Gurus in the first three Yugas and is being now similarly transmitted. Towards the end of the Dvāparayuga, and at the beginning of the Kali age, merciful Śiva impelled by compassion for humanity bound in the toils of ignorance, divided the Tantra-śāstra, which is unlimited knowledge, into three sets of sixty-four parts each, according to the necessity of different Adhikārīs, and then told them to Gaṇapati and Kārtikeya the two beloved sons of Pārvatī. They repeated these

Tantras to Ṛṣis of Siddhāśramas, and these last, in their turn, told them to their own disciples. Of the Ṛṣis who knew Āgama the chief was Dattātreya, an incarnation of Viṣṇu. At the beginning of the Kalpa the ancient Brahmavidyā contained in the Āgama appeared from out the Parameṣti-guru who is Mahābrahmavidyā and exists in man's heart unlimited and imperishable. If Sādhanā is done according to the instructions of a Sadguru it becomes visible in the Sādhaka's heart. Upāsanā, in the Vaidik form, predominated in the Satyayuga. In those days Brāhmaṇas, and other twice born castes, impelled by a desire for wealth, progeny and so forth used to worship Indra, Agni, Vāyu, Sūrya, Soma, Varuṇa and other Devas presiding over particular Śaktis of Parameśvara in whom all Śaktis reside. But desire-free Brahmarṣis and Maharṣis did Sādhanā of Brahmavidyā the full and perfect Śakti. And so we see in the tenth Maṇdala (१२५) of the Ṛgveda-Saṁhitā that Mahādevī appeared in the heart of the daughter of Maharṣi Āṁbhṛṇī and so told the true nature of Brahmavidyā to Ṛṣis. This is the Devīsūkta full of Advaitatattva, the Hymn telling of the true nature of Brahma-vidyā in the Veda. In the Tretā and other Yugas the Brāhmaṇas and other twice-born devoted to the Karmakāṇda used to perform Yajñas and so forth, according to the Smritiśāstras of Manu and others. But Brahmarṣi Vaṣiṣṭha (in Cīnācāra) Rājarṣi Viśvāmitra (see Gandharva-Tantra, First Patala), Videharāja Janaka, Bhṛgurāma the son of Jamadagni (see Kālīkulasarvasva), Śrī Rāmacandra and other high-souled men were worshippers of Brahmavidyā the full and perfect Śakti. Again in the Dvāparayuga, despite the existence of Vaidik and Smārta cults, the Agnihotra Yajña and other rites used to be performed according to the Purāṇas. But high-souled Śrīkriṣna the son of Vasudeva (see Rādhā-Tantra, Devī Bhāgavata and Mahābhārata, Anuśāsana Parva, Ch. 14), the five Pāndavas namely Yudhiṣthira and others (Virāta Parva, Ch. 6) the high-souled Rājarṣi Bhīshma, the great Muni Vedavyāsa, high souled Śukadeva, Asita, Devala and Brahmarṣis such as Durvāsā were worshippers of Mahāvidyā the perfect Śakti. Of this the Mahābhārata and other books provide particular proofs. In the present Kaliyuga also the ten Śaṁskāras such as marriage and so forth of the twice born, and the obsequial ceremonies such as Śrāddha are performed according to Vaidik ritual. Smṛti governs Cāndrāyana and other matters relating to Āśrama and legal affairs such as inheritance. The autummal Durgāpūjā and other Vratas are performed according to the Purāṇas. But initiation, Upāsanā of Brahman with Śakti and various practices of Yoga are done according to the ritual of the Āgama Śāstra.

This latter is of three kinds according to the prevalence of the Guṇas namely Tantra, Yāmala and Dāmara. There are in all 192 Āgamas current, namely 64 each in Aśvakrāntā, Rathakrāntā, and Viṣnukrāntā. Many Tantras were lost in Buddhist and Mahommedan times and the few which still remain with Sādhakas in different parts of the country are not shown by them to any but to their disciples, so that these also are about to be lost. The late Rasika-

Mohana-Chattopādhyāya, with great effort and cost, saved some of these and the English Arthur Avalon has done the same and I hope yet others will in future be rescued by him.

In the Yoginī-Tantra Īśvara says to Devī that the difference between Vedas and Agamas is like that between Jīva and Ātmā, that is between Jīva covered with Avidyā and Īśvara who is full of Vidyā. Indra and other Devas who used to be worshipped as Īśvaras in Yajñas held under the Karmakāṇḍa or Saṁhitā of the Vedas are, in Tantra-śāstra, worshipped as the Presiding Devatās of the Dikpālinī Śakti of Her who is all Śaktis (Sarvaśakti-svarūpiṇī). The three Īśvaras Brahmā, Viṣṇu and Rudra of the Vedas and Purāṇas are in Tantra-śāstra the presiding Devatās of the creative, preservative, and dissolving Śaktis of Mahādevī. As such they are worshipped as the supports of the couch of the Mahādevī. She in the Devīgītā says that 'Brahmā, Viṣṇu, Īśvara, Sadāśiva are five Mahāpreta at my Feet. They are constituted of the five Bhūta and represent the five different elements of matter.' 'I however' She says 'am unmanifested consciousness (Chit) and in every way beyond them.'

Again the Veda says 'All this is verily Brahman.' Despite this Mahāvākya, various distinctions are made, such as those of caste, Adhikāra of men and women and so forth. So a male Brāhmaṇa may say Vaidik Mantras but not Brāhmaṇa women. Distinction was again made between objects as between the water of the Ganges and a well. All such distinctions are wholly opposed to the Spirit of the Great Word (Mahāvākya). The Tantra-śāstra says that the supreme Brahman is both subtle and gross. In dependence on the truth of this Mahāvākya Tāntrik Sādhakas purify wine which is 'not to be taken and drunk' according to Veda. Considering it to be as holy as nectar, they offer it into the mouth of Kulakuṇdalinī who is Consciousness itself (Citsvarūpinī). Again, in accordance with Veda, the Tantra holds food to be sacred and knowing that food is Brahman ordains the offering of it to Mahādevī. This offered food is Mahāprasāda and very holy and rare even for Devas, and whether it be brought by a Caṇdāla, or even fallen from the mouth of a dog. The Vedas and Smṛti say that the Caṇdāla and other low castes are untouchable. On touching them one must bathe, do Aghamarshana and so forth. But the Tantra-Śāstra says that even a Caṇdālā, who has a knowledge of Kula doctrine and Brahman, is superior to a Brāhmaṇa who does not know Brahman. The Tantra-Śāstra again says that during the Cakra all castes are equal. Since all are children of the one Mother of the World, no distinctions should be made at the time of worshipping Her. It is on this Tāntrik authority that no caste distinctions are observed in the matter of eating and so forth in the Virajākṣetra of Śrī Śrī Vimalā Devī. The Veda again prohibits the performance of Yajña or worship after the taking of food. Tantra-Śāstra however says that one should not worship Kālika whilst suffering from hunger or thirst otherwise She becomes angry. That is since Śiva and Jīva are really one it is futile to worship the Paramātmā saying 'I offer Naivedya' when the Jīva, who is one with It, is in want of food and drink. Smṛti again, which explains Veda ordains that the Shālagrama stone which represents Nārāyaṇa should not be touched or worshipped by any but Brāhmaṇas. On the other hand, the Tantra-Śāstra ordains that the Bānaliṅga representation of the Brahman may be touched and worshipped not only by Brāhmaṇas but by Śūdras, Caṇḍālas and women. In fact the Karmakāṇḍa of Veda contains many such ordinances opposed to Brahman-knowledge. For this reason Bhagavān Śrīkṛṣṇa has said in the Gītā that the Vedas are concerned with objects constituted of the three Guṇas (Triguṇaviṣaya) and bids Arjuna to free himself of the Guṇas. He says the Veda contains the Karmakāṇḍa but that he who seeks the Brahman-state above the Guṇas should abandon the Karmakāṇḍa and perform Sādhanā according to Śāstra by which Liberation is gained. In spite however of differences in worship and practice both Veda and Tantra Śāstras are one in holding that there can be no Liberation without Tattvajñāna. In the Nirvāṇa-Tantra Śiva says 'Oh Devī, there is no Liberation without Tattvajñāna.' According to Veda, a Sādhaka, in order to become fit for Nirvāṇa, must have first accomplished the fourfold Sādhanā. He must have acquired the faith that Brahman is alone everlasting, and have no desire for happiness either on earth or in heaven. He must possess the six virtues, Śama, Dama and so forth, and must long for Liberation. He then discusses (Vicāra) and ponders on the Mahāvākya 'That thou art' (Tat tvam asi), and thus realizing the unity of Paramātmā and Jīvātmā, attains the knowledge 'He I am' (So'ham).

In Tāntrik Upāsanā the Jñānakāṇḍa is mingled with the Karmakāṇḍa. The Agama teaches the ignorant Paśu, steeped in dualism, Vīrabhāva Sādhanā in which dualism and non-dualism are mingled. It thus endeavours to raise them to the divine state of Jivanmuktas, the state of pure Monism. Manu says 'Know dualists to be Paśus. Non-dualists are Brāhmaṇas.' Rudrayāmala says that Vīrabhāva is revealed for the development of Jñāna. After perfecting Jñāna and attainment of Brahmasiddhi, the Sādhaka becomes Devatā in a pure state of Sattva. The Vedanta and philosophic Śāstras are replete with instructions and arguments touching non-dualism. But they do not indicate the path by which one can be in actual practice non-dualistic. For this reason we see Vedāntic Pandits deeming it unclean to touch a low caste man such as a Śūdra. They also observe endless distinctions as to what should or should not be eaten, and what should and should not be offered to Devatā. Tantra-Śāstra however says that non-dualistic Bhāva (Bhāvādvaita) should be accompanied by non-dualistic action (Kriyādvaita). The Yoga-vāṣiṣtha (Rāmāyaṇa) says that to the Muni who realizes non-dualism (Advaita) in Bhāva, in Kriyā, and in objects (Dravya) in all these three matters the world, seems but a dream.

According to the instruction of Tantra-Śāstra the Sādhaka rises in the early hours of the morning, and sitting on his bed, meditates as follows: 'I am the Devī and none other. I am that Brahman who knows not grief. I am a form of Being-Consciousness-Bliss, Whose true nature is eternal Liberation.' Again at noon sitting at worship he does Bhutaśuddhi, and therein merging the 24 Tattvas beginning with earth in Paramātmā and thinking of the Paramātmā and Jīvātmā as one he meditates: 'He I am.' Gandharva-Tantra says that, after due obeisance to the Guru, the wise Sādhaka should think 'He I am' and thus unite Jīvātmā and Paramātmā. In all Sthūla-Dhyāna of Mahāvidyās, forming part of daily worship, Tantra-Śāstra everywhere enjoins meditation on the Mahādevī as not different from, but one with, the Sādhaka's Ātmā. The Kālī-Tantra says that, after meditating as enjoined, the Sādhaka should worship the Devī as Ātmā. 'He I am' (So'ham). Kubjikā-Tantra says that the Sādhaka should think of his Ātmā as one with Her. Nīla-Tantra in the Dhyāna of Tārā says that meditation should be done on one's own Ātmā as one with the Saviour-goddess (Tārinī). In Gandharva-Tantra Mahādevī says, as regards the Dhyāna of Tripurasundarī, that the Man who meditates on the unattached, attributeless, and pure Ātmā which is Tripurā as one with, and not different from, his own Ātmā becomes himself Her (Tanmaya). One should become Her by ever thinking 'She I am' (Sā'ham). Again in the Kālī-kula-sarvasva Śiva says that whoever meditates on the Guru and recites the Hymn of the spouse of Śiva and thinks of Kālikā's Ātmā as one with his own Ātmā is Śrī Sadāsiva. Similarly Kulārṇava Tantra says 'The body is the temple of Devatā and the Jima is Deva Sadāsiva.' Let the Sādhaka give up his ignorance as the offering (Nirmālya, which is thrown away) and worship with the thought and feeling 'He I am.' It is not only at times of worship and so forth that the Sādhaka is enjoined to meditate on Her who is Paramātmā as one with his own Ātmā. Śiva teaches that our thought and feeling should be non-dualistic in all that we do, in eating, in walking and so forth. Hence in the Gandharva-Tantra Śiva says 'I am both the Deva and the food offered to Him, the flower and perfume and all else. I am the Deva. There is none other than Me. It is I who worship the Deva and I am also Deva of Devas.' Again it is ordained that at the time of taking Kāraṇa (wine) and the rest they should be offered to the Fire of Consciousness in one's own heart, uttering the Mantra, and thinking that Kula-Kuṇdalinī extends to the tip of his tongue, let the Sādhaka say: 'The liquid shines. I am the Light. I am Brahman. She I am. I offer Āhuti to my own Self Svāhā.' He who does Sādhanā of the Mahāvidyā in Vīrāchāra with such Advaitabhāva attains by Her Grace to Divyabhāva, and with the thought 'I am Brahman' becomes liberated whilst living, and on death is one with Mahādevī. In the Devigitā Śrī Śrī Devī says 'He becomes Myself because both are one.' Again the Mahānirvāṇa-Tantra enjoins a similar non-dualistic feeling in the Mantra to be said when taking the Dravya (wine). 'The ladle is Brahman, the offering is Brahman, the fire is Brahman, the offering is made by Brahman and to Brahman he goes who places all his actions in Brahman.'

Saccidānanda Mahāvidyā, in undistinguishable union of Śiva and Śakti, can alone be worshipped with such non-dualism of feeling. Although Tāntrik worshippers are divided into five communities namely Śākta, Śaiva, Vaiṣṇava, Gāṇapatya, Saura the first alone are all Dvijas since all worshippers of Sāvitrī (Gāyatrī) the Mother of the Veda belong to the Śākta community. The Mātṛkābheda-Tantra says 'Sāvitrī the Mother of the Veda was born of the sweat of Kālī's body. That Devī grants the threefold fruit and is Śakti of Brahman.' Sādhakas belonging to the other four communities worship their respective male Devatās associating with them their Śaktis. Thus the Śaivas worship Śiva under the names Umā-Maheśvara, Śiva-Durgā, Kālī Śaṁkara, Arddhanārīśvara and so forth. The Vaiṣṇavas worship Viṣṇu under the names, Rādhā-Kṛṣṇa, Lakṣmī-Nārāyaṇa, Sītā-Rāma, Śrī-Hari and so forth. In the Nirvāna-Tantra Śri Kṛṣṇa says 'To those who do Japa of Rādhā first and then Kṛṣṇa to such I, of a surety, grant a happy lot even now and here.' By uttering the name Sītā-Rama (Sītā coming first) one utters the Tāra of Mahādevī, and for this reason it is also called Tāraka-Brahma. The Sauras perform their worship. with the Mantra 'Obeisance to Śrī Sūrya accompanied by the Śakti who reveals.' Moreover the Māyā Bīja (Hrīm), which is the Praṇava of Devī, is added to the Mūlamantra by every sect. This clearly shows that all these five sects are directly or indirectly worshippers of the Brahman who is Śiva-Śakti (Śivaśaktyātmaka) both in his Nirguṇa and Saguṇa aspects. Kaivalyopaniṣad says 'By meditation on the three-eyed, blue-throated serene Lord (Prabhu) Parameśvara, who is without beginning, middle and end, who is one and pervades all things, who is wonderful, Cidānanda Itself, accompanied by Umā, the Muni goes to the Source of all being (Bhūtayoni) to the Witness of all, who is beyond all darkness.' Hence in the Tantra-Śāstra, Śiva has said that the Śiva-śakti-Tattva is the cause of Tattvajñāna and therefore Japa should be done by a Mantra in which they are united. That is one attains Tattvajñāna, which is liberation, by worshipping Brahman as Mother and Father. All Mantras being composed of Śiva and Śakti one should meditate on Śiva-Śakti as being one. In the Tantra Śāstra also Śiva has said that there is no difference between them who are inseparably connected (Avinābhāvasaṁbandha). He who is Śiva is also Śakti and She who is Śakti is also Śiva. Fatherhood and Motherhood are merely distinctions of name. In reality they stand for one and the same thing. The Tantra Śāstra again says that Śakti, Maheśvara, Brahman all denote the same Being. Male, female, neuter are verbal and not real distinctions. Śakti, Maheśvara, Brahman; all three denote the one eternal Mahāvidyā who is Saccidānanda. Although the Mahāvidyā is in truth Nirguṇa and eternal, She assumes various Māyik forms, varying according to the Guṇas, for the fruition of the desires of Sādhakas. It is said in Candi that She ever appears to fulfil the purposes of Devas, and at such time She, who is Truth eternal, is commonly said to he generated. In the Devyāgama it is said: 'Mahāmāyā who is Citrūpā and Parabrahmasvarūpinī assumes by Her grace towards Sādhakas various forms.' We may meditate on Mahādevī as either female or male, for these terms may be attributed to any gross body. They cannot however be attributed to Her in so far as She is Saccidānanda. Sādhakas of Śakti worship Brahman as Mother, for in the world the mother-aspect alone of Her who is Brahman is fully manifested. In the Yāmala, Śiva says:—'Devī may, My Beloved, be thought of as female or male, or the Saccidānandarūpiṇī may be thought of as Niṣkala-Brahman. But in truth She is neither a female, male, neuter being, nor an inanimate thing. But like the term Kalpavallī (a word in feminine gender denoting tree) feminine terms are attributed to Her.'

In fact the main cause of the birth and nourishment of men and animals is their respective mothers. Their fathers are merely helpers (Sahakārī). Every Jīva on issuing from his mother's womb, lives on her milk, and receives his first initiation with the Mantra 'Mā' (Mother). The first preceptor (Adiguru) of every man is his mother. She is his visible Devatā. His first lessons are learnt of her. It is the mark also of the Earth to generate and nourish all Jivas, like a mother, by producing for them all kinds of fruits and grains and holding them in her bosom. Hence we are not wrong in saying that the world is full of the Mother.

In mathematics zero has no value and is merely an empty formless (Nirākāra) thing, indicative of infinity until it is joined to an integer. But when joined to the figure 1 it converts it into 10. Similarly when She who is formless Brahman is joined to Her own Prakṛti, consisting of the three Guṇas, spoken of in Śruti as 'the unborn one, red, black, and white,' then She assumes for the fruition of the Sādhaka's desires ten different forms (Daśamahāvidyā) whose variety is due to difference in the proportions of the three Gunas. There are the ten Mahāvidyās who are Śiva and Śakti (Śivaśaktimayī). These ten forms are Kālī and Tārā, the Mahāvidyā Ṣodaśī, Bhuvaneśvarī, Bhairavī, Chinnamastā, Dhūmāvatī, the Vidyā Bagalā, the Siddhavidyā Mātaṅgī, and Kamalā. Some Tantras mention eighteen Mahāvidyā, but these are forms of the ten with slight variations. Of the ten Mahāvidyās, Kālī is Śuddha-sattva-guṇa-pradhānā, Nirvikārā, Nirguṇa-brahma-svarūpa-prakāśikā. It is this primordial form which alone directly gives Kaivalya. In Yoginī-Tantra Devī says 'Now see my form (Rūpa) which is Brahmānanda and supreme. Listen, this form is the supreme state (Paramadhāma) in the form of Kālī. There is no Brahman-form higher than this.' In Kamadhenu-Tantra Śiva says 'In the void is Kālī who grants Kaivalya'. Tara is Sattva-guṇātmikā and Tattvavidyādāyini; Ṣodaśi (Mahātripura-sundarī), Bhuvaneśvarī and Chinnamastā are Rajah-pradhānā and Sattva-guṇātmikā and hence they grant Gauṇamukti in the form of Heaven (Svarga) Aiśvarya and so forth. The forms of Dhūmāvatī, Bagalā, Mātaṅgī and Kamalā are Tamah-pradhāna and hence their Sādhanā is done in Ṣatkarma, such as causing death to others and so forth. In short all the ten forms of Mahādevī give Enjoyment and Liberation directly or indirectly.

The forms of the Mahāvidyā are divided into two groups namely the Kālīkula and Śrikula. So Niruttara-Tantra says that 'Kālī, Tara, Raktakālī, Bhuvanā, Mardinī, Triputā, Tvaritā, Durgā and Vidyā Pratyaṅgīrā belong to the Kālīkula. And to the Śrīkula belong Sundarī, Bhairavī, Bālā, Bagalā, Kamalā, Dhūmāvatī, Mātaṅgī, Vidyā, Svapnāvatī and Mahāvidyā Madhumatī. Of all the Siddhavidyās Dakṣinā is, O my beloved, the Cause (Prakṛti)'.

Kālī-kula is for the worship of Jñānīs in Divya and Vīrabhāva, and Śrī-kula is for the worship of Karmins in Divya, Vīra and Paśu-Bhāvas. The Tantra-Śāstra gives an account of the Mantras, Yantras, mode of worship and so forth for all the ten or eighteen Mahāvidyās. But almost all Tāntrik writings hymn the greatness of, and give the highest place to, Kālikā the first

Mahāvidyā for the others are but different forms of Brahmarūpiṇī Kālikā. The Nigama-Kalpataru says 'Of all castes the Brāhmaṇa is the highest. Amongst all Sādhakas the Śākta is the highest. Of Śāktas he is the chief who does Japa of the Kālīmantra.' Picchilā-Tantra also says 'of all the Mantras of the Devas that of Kālikā is the best. Even the vilest can become Jīvanmukta simply through this Mantra.' In Yoginī-Tantra, Śiva says 'This Vidyā Kālikā is Mahā-Mahā-Brahma Vidyā, through whom even the worst may attain Nirvāṇa. Even Brahmā, Viṣṇu, and Maheśvara are her worshippers. She who is Kālī the supreme Vidyā, is Tārā also. The notion of a difference between them has given rise to various Mantras.' Again the Kāmākhyā-Tantra says 'Oh Parameśvari, seven lakhs of Mahāvidyās remain hidden. Of them all Ṣodaśi is said to be the most sublime. But Oh Devī, the Mother of the world, Kālikā is the mother even of Her.' Niruttara-Tantra says 'Without knowledge of Śakti, Oh Devī, there is no nirvāṇa. That Śakti is Dakṣiṇa Kālī who is the own form of all Vidyās (Sarvavidyārūpiṇī).' The Yāmala again says 'As is Kālī so is Tārā and so are Chinnā and Kullukā. Oh Devī, thou, who art the supreme Kālikā, art also the Marti which is composed of these four. In the Vaidik system Sagnika (fire-maintaining) Brāhmaṇas achieved their ends by the offering of oblations to the seven lolling tongues of fire named Kālī, Karālī, Manojavā, Sulohitā, Sudhūmravarṇā, Sphuliṅginī and Devī Viśvaruci' (1st Saptaka, 2nd Khaṇda, 4th Sūtra). [1]

Another important characteristic, of the Tantra-Śāstra remains to be mentioned. Although this Scripture is very liberal in matters of practice and worship and does not recognize distinctions of caste and so forth, it has yet repeatedly, enjoined Sādhakas to keep this Ācāra hidden from ignorant Paśus. Of Kaulas it says that 'they are at heart Śāktas, outwardly Śaivas, and in gatherings Vaiṣṇavas'. It also contains injunctions such as that the teaching should be kept as secret as one would the knowledge of one's mother's illicit love, and that if it is given out the Sādhaka's purpose is frustrated and so forth. In the Gandharva-Tantra, Śiva says that only such men as are without dualism, have controlled their passions and are devoted to Brahman are entitled to this Śāstra. 'He alone is entitled, who is a believer, pure, self-controlled, without dualism who lives in Brahman, speaks of Brahman, is devoted to Brahman, takes refuge in Brahman, who is free from all feeling of enmity against others, and who is ever engaged in doing good to all beings. Others are not true Sādhakas (Brahmasādhaka). It should not be told to Paśus, to those who are insincere, or to men of shallow knowledge.' For this reason Śiva has used symbols in the teaching of all Dhyānas, Mantras, Yantras, and modes of Sādhanā of Devas and Devīs. The meaning of these symbols is not known to any but the Sadguru. Hence the secret mysteries are unintelligible even to the learned without the grace of the Guru. In the Kulārṇava-Tantra, Śiva says 'There are many Gurus who know the Veda, the Śāstras and so forth. But, Oh Devī, rare is the Guru who knows the meaning of the supreme Tattva'. Hence in order to know the true meaning of the

Dhyānas and so forth, there is no other means than to seek refuge with the Guru who knows the meaning of all Agamas.

It is owing to ignorance of the true nature of Devatā that even Brahmavidyā, who is subtler than the most subtle and Consciousness Itself, seems to be a gross thing. Even learned men do not shrink from saying that this Brahmamayī, whose desires are fully realized (Pūrṇakāmā) is fond of offerings of blood, flesh and so forth. In the Jñānasaṁkalinī-Tantra, Śiva says, 'Agni is the Deva of the twice born. The Devatā of Munis is in their hearts. Men of small intelligence worship images. To the wise, Devatā is everywhere.' That is Karmin Brāhmaṇas worship Agni as Īśvara, Yogis see the Devatā in their own hearts, men of small intelligence (that is compared with the others) worship the Devatā in images, and high-souled seers of the Tattva see Brahman everywhere. In fact much as a teacher shows his little students, small globes and maps, in order to make them understand the nature of the great earth, so Gurus counsel Sādhakas of no great intelligence and of inferior Adhikāra to meditate on Sthūla forms in images and pictures so that their wandering minds may be rested, and they may learn the true aspects of Devatā. Unfortunately however, ignorant men consider the Sthūla form to be the true aspect of the Devatā. In the Kulārṇava-Tantra, Śiva says that some meditate on the Sthūla to still the mind, which, when so stilled, can fix itself on the Sūkṣma. The Sādhaka should first learn from the Guru what quality or action each limb of the image represents, and should then practise meditation on the subtle, otherwise the gross form will itself, become for him mere earth or stone. In Kubjikā-Tantra Śiva says 'Oh Lady of Maheśa. One should meditate on the Formless (here used in the sense as opposed to forms of images, etc.) along with the form. It is by constant practice, Oh Devī, that one realizes the formless.'

Hence Sādhakas who desire Liberation should always think of the Svarūpatattva of Brahmavidyā-Kālikā. Of this Svarūpa the Devī says in Mahābhāgavata: 'Those who long for Liberation should, in order to gain freedom from the bonds of the body, meditate on that aspect (Rūpa) of Mine which is the supreme Light (Jyotih), Sūkṣma, and Niṣkala, Nirguṇa, the all-pervading unbeginning, non-dual sole Cause which is Saccidānanda Itself. This is the Svarūpa of the Devī which is beyond all mind and speech.'

The Mārkaṇḍeya-Purāṇa says, 'The Mahāmāyā is Niṣkalā, Nirguṇā, endless, undecaying, unthinkable, formless and both eternal (Nityā) and transient (Anityā)', that is, Mahāmāyā Kālikā is free from Kalā (Māyā) and free from Guṇas, without end, imperishable, eternal, and not transient as is the world (Jagat), formless, and hence, as such, is not the object of meditation. In the Kūrma-Purāṇa, Viṣṇu in the form of a Tortoise says that the Supreme Devī is Nirguṇā, pure, white, stainless, free from all duality and realizable by the Ātmā only. This state of Hers is attainable only by Jñāna. In the Kāmadā-Tantra Śiva says 'That eternal Kālī who is supreme Brahman is one without a second either male or female. She has neither form, Ādhāra, or Upādhi. She is sinless and imperishable Sacchidānanda, the Great Brahman.' She who is eternal Brahman has neither appearance (Āvirbhāva), nor disappearance (Tirobhāva), and being all-pervading, She cannot be said, like other Devas and Devīs, to reside in any particular Loka. Thus Brahmā resides in Brahmaloka, Viṣṇu in Viṣṇuloka, Rudra in Kailāsa and Śrī Kṛṣṇa in Goloka, but Mahādevī is always and everywhere equally present; though for the fulfilment of the desires of Sādhakas, She appears in particular forms in their minds and hearts. It is clear therefore that her Sthūla aspect is Māyā-made (Māyāmaya) and transient (Anitya). For this reason Śiva, in the Gandharva-Tantra, says, 'That aspect (Rūpa) of the Devī which is the Supreme Bliss and the Great Cause of the worlds neither appears nor disappears'. In the Kulārṇava-Tantra, Śiva says, 'It neither rises nor sets, nor grows nor decays; It shines Itself and makes others shine without any help. This aspect is without condition (Anavasthā) and is being only (Sattāmātrā) and unknowable to the senses (Agocara).' That is, the Svarūpa aspect of the Māhādevī who is Supreme Bliss is the root-cause of this world of three Gunas. This aspect has no appearance or disappearance and no growth or decay. 'It is self-manifest and manifests all other objects. It is beyond the states of waking, dreams, and sleep. It is unattainable by speech and mind and is Being itself.'

In fact just as fire which, though pervading all objects, does not show its power of burning and lighting, and cannot be put to use for cooking and so forth, until it has been generated by the friction of two objects, so although the Cinmayī is all-pervading, She does not become visible nor does She grant one's desire without the action of Sādhanā. Again just as the Sun itself, motionless in the distant Heavens, by its rays draws moisture from the earth, so the Mahādevī, who is the abode of all Śaktis, though in Herself changeless (Nirvikārā) creates (and the like) the world by means of the eight Śaktis, Brahmāṇī, Vaiṣṇavi, Māheśvarī and other Devatās, presiding as her creative and other Śaktis. For this reason in the Yantra of Mahādevī Kālikā (see Kālikopaniṣad) the Sādhaka worships the fifteen Śaktis Kālī and others in the fifteen corners, the eight Śaktis Brāhmī and others on the eight petals, the eight Bhairavas and Vatukas Asitānga and the rest at the edges of the eight petals, the four Devatās, Viṣṇu and others, at the four corners of the Yantra, and the ten Dikpālas, Indra and others, in the ten directions as being the rays of Kālikā who is Herself a mass of pure light (Tejoghana). The Mahādevī is worshipped as the Marti consisting of Śiva-Śakti (Śivaśaktimaya) in the Bindu at the centre of the Yantra.

Although the Āgama-Śāstra, which grants Advaitabhāva and educes Tattvajñāna, has been revealed by all-merciful Śrī Śrī Bhairava and Bhairavī, it is still unknown to a mass of people. Many in fact to-day despise the Tantra because it contains Virācāra and Kulācāra, and some even refuse to admit that it is a Dharmaśāstra at all. If they had read the Tantra-Śāstra intelligently and learned its principles from Sādhakas truly versed in it, they would have realized how mistaken were their notions of it and, instead of despising it, would certainly have admitted that this Śāstra is the only means of Liberation for the undisciplined, weakminded and short-lived. Seeing that wine, flesh, fish are consumed and sexual intercourse takes place in the world at large I am myself unable to understand why many people should shudder at the Sādhanā of Pañca-makāra to be found in the Tantra-Śāstra. Do these acts become blameable only if made a part of worship (Upāsanā)?

All know that Ghee which nourishes and promotes longevity causes serious stomach-disease and even death if taken in too large quantities, whilst snake-poison, which kills, will yet cure and lengthen the life of a dying delirious man, if it be purified and given under suitable conditions with a cold bath, a diet of whey, and so forth. Similarly the Great Physician (Vaidyanātha) Himself has prescribed the Mantra of Ādyāśakti possessed of all Śaktis, and the invigorating Pañca-makāra as Sādhanā suitable for the cure of the malady of Existence (Bhavaroga) of the sinful Jivas of this dark Kali age, and as a means whereby they may attain the supreme state full of eternal bliss, imperishable and immortal. All classes of physicians prescribe the use of wine, fish and flesh in measured quantities for the acquisition of strength by patients who are weak and have a low vitality. On that account the medical science does not deserve to be hated. Similarly the Tantra-Śāstra does not deserve to be blamed for prescribing the Pañca-makāra for the Liberation of Jivas suffering from the disease of worldly existence. Śiva has nowhere said that Sādhakas of Śakti should always drink wine, always slaughter animals and eat their flesh and always enjoy women, and that thus they will attain Liberation. On the contrary, He has counselled various means for checking excesses in these matters, and He has in particular controlled licence by making these acts part of the worship of Īśvara. It is the degraded conduct of a number of great Paśus who pretend to be Sādhakas which is the cause of the public dislike for, and hatred of, the Tantra-Śāstra. In the Mahānirvāṇa-Tantra Śrī Sadāśiva says 'Wine is Tara the Saviour in liquid form (Dravamayī). It saves Jivas destroying dangers and disease, and grants both Enjoyment and Liberation. But wine if drunk in contravention of rule (Vidhi), destroys the intelligence, reputation, wealth and life of men. Even a Kaula who has received Abhiṣeka an hundred times is to be deemed a Paśu and without the pale of Kuladharma if he is addicted to excessive drinking.' In the Kulārṇava, Śiva says 'Oh My Beloved, he who kills animals for self-satisfaction in contravention of gastric ordinance (Avidhānena) will dwell in a terrible Hell for as many days as there are hairs on the body of the animal.' These utterances of Śiva clearly show that He has nowhere ordained the free use of Pañca-makāra by people in general. He has ordained Virācāra or Kulācāra only for Sādhakas of the Nivṛtti path who long for Liberation. Such Sādhakas, free from duality (Nirvikalpa) as they are, wish to see the Saccidānanda aspect of the Mahādevī, and Śiva has prescribed the Pañca-makāra to enable them to realize the Ānanda aspect. Just as a man who knows not sweetness is given sugar or honey to eat, so the Sādhaka is made to taste the fleeting objective (Vīṣaya) bliss (Ānanda) of Pañca-makāra so that, thus controlling his six enemies for the time being, he may have a notion of the Eternal Brahman-bliss (Brahmānanda): This momentary taste of eternal Brahman-bliss makes the Liberation-desiring Sādhaka eager for and industrious to gain it. But after the attainment of this natural (Sahaja) Brahman-bliss he no more longs for the five Makāras and becomes gradually devoted to Divyācāra. If a Sādhaka takes wine in a limited way, after purification, the outgoing of his senses is weakened, and the mind or inner sense is stilled so that he is thus fitted for Sūkṣma-Dhyāna. For this reason wine is called cause (Kāraṇa). In the Kulārṇava-Tantra, Shiva says, 'Ānanda is the Self (Rūpa) of Brahman and that exists in the body. Wine is its revealer and is hence drunk by Yogis. Wine and flesh are taken with Brahmajñāna for the satisfaction of all Devas, and whoever partakes of them for self-gratification is a sinner.' That is Sādhakas do Sādhanā with Pañca-makāra for the satisfaction of the Devatās whom they worship and the development of Brahmajñāna in their hearts; but whoever takes them for his own enjoyment is doomed to a terrible hell as a great sinner. Śiva has also said in the Kulārṇava, 'One reaches heaven by the very things which may lead to Hell.' The fifth Makāra, that is, sexual intercourse, is the root-cause of the creation of the world of Jivas. All Jivas, be they Devatās, men, beasts, birds, fish, insects or flies, are produced by the sexual union of their respective parents. In this world every male is an individualised (Vyaṣṭībhūta) aspect of Shiva, the Ādipuruṣa, and Caṇdī says, 'all females in all the worlds' are part of the Mahāśakti. The Kūrma-Purāṇa says, 'The Mahādevī is Herself One, present in many parts or divisions (Anekavibhāgasthā), beyond Māyā, absolutely pure, Mahāmāyā, Iśvarī, eternal, stainless (Nirañjana), ancient, consciousness (Cinmayī), the First Puruṣa (Ādipuruṣa) of all Puruṣas.' The Gandharva-Tantra says, 'The male form (Puṁso rūpam) the female form, and any other good form—all this is undoubtedly Her supreme form (Paramam rūpam).' One Brahman, becoming dual, appears as Śiva and Śakti, and that aspect in which there is union of Śiva and Śakti is the true aspect of Saccidānanda Brahman. It is from this aspect of Blissful (Ānandamaya) union that the world is created, and for that reason men and all other creatures ever seek happiness. The Bliss of the reproductive power of males and females manifests in their bodies only at the time of sexual union. At this time ignorant men remain intent only on gratifying their passion, but Sādhakas, possessed of the knowledge of Kula, then meditate on the Yoga-blissful (Yogānanda) form (Mūrti) of Śiva and Śakti present in the hearts of males and females and, calling to mind the meaning (Artha) of the Mantra of their Iṣtadevatā, do Japa of it. In the Kālīkulasarvasva, Śrī Sadāśiva says, 'By doing Japa of Mantra and by adoration of Bhagavatī, the consort of Śiva, at times of sexual union, a man becomes, like Śuka, free from all sins.' In another place He says, 'The consort of Śiva should be worshipped by becoming Śiva.' True Śakti-sādhanā consists in considering all girls and women, old and young, and of all castes, as the visible forms of one's own Iṣtadevatā and (according to one's means) worshipping them with clothes, ornaments and so forth; or bowing to them as mothers with the Iṣtamantra in mind and not treating them with neglect or contempt under any circumstance. In the Kaulāvalī-Tantra, Śiva says, 'One should make obeisance on seeing a young woman of a Kaula family. One should bow to any female, be she a young girl, or flushed with youth, or be she old, be she beautiful or ugly, good, or wicked. One should never deceive, speak ill of, or do ill to, a woman and one should never strike her. All such acts prevent the attainment of Siddhi.'

At the present time a measured use of wine, flesh and so forth and a thorough respect for woman as for the Devatā are particularly seen in the civilized society of the West. Satisfied at this, the Mahādevī, who is the Queen of Queens, has granted to the people of the West the light of science and sovereignty over the whole world. Śrīmat Ādinātha Mahākāla has, in the 'Karpūrādi Stotra' called the Svarūpa-Stotra, briefly described the Mantra, Yantra, Dhyāna and Sādhanā of Śrīmatī Dakṣiṇa-Kālikā who is Parabrahman (Parabrahmarūpiṇī). This Supreme Tattva is hard to attain even by such Īśvaras as Brahmā, Viṣṇu and Rudra. Mahākāla Himself says, 'Neither Dhātā nor Īśa nor Hari knows Thy Supreme Tattva.'

However, in accordance with the teachings of my Paramaguru, Mahāmahopādhyāya and most worshipful Rāmānanda Svāmī Siddhāntapañcānana, the crest-gem of Tāntrikas, now gathered to the feet of Śiva, I write this Svarūpa commentary under the name of 'Vimalānandadāyinī,' of this Karpūrādi Stotra, in consonance with the views of Tantra and other Śāstras.

PRAYER

AT THE FEET OF ŚRĪ ŚRĪ KĀLIKĀ

May the Mahā-Devī who is called Kālikā,
Because She is without beginning or end,
Whose Body is imagined to be blue of colour,
Because like the blue sky She pervades the World,
And because She is Cidghanā [2] Sattvaguṇamayī
Who is imagined to be black
Because She is colourless and above the coloured Guṇas,
Whose hair is dishevelled (Muktakeśī)
Because though Herself changeless She binds infinite numbers of Jivas by bonds of Māyā, symbolized by Her dishevelled hair and because She makes liberated (Mukta) Brahmā, Viṣṇu and Maheśvara who are Keśa, [3]

Who is imagined as having the Sun, Moon and Fire as Her three eyes,
Because as the Virad, the Witness of the world past, present and future She sees everything,
Who is pictured as wearing the dead bodies of two boys as Her ear-ornaments,
Because as said in Āgama and Nigama the childlike and unperturbed (Nir-

vikāra) Sādhaka is very dear to Her, who being the sole Creatrix, Preserver and Destructress of infinite millions of Worlds, has on Her Body the mark of the Yoni signifying creation, full and high breasts denoting preservation, and a terrible visage signifying the withdrawal of all things, Who is said to have large teeth, and a lolling tongue and to hold in Her hand a cup made of human skull,

Because the Cinmayī Mahādevī drinks the wine of delusion arising from the Tamas Guṇa of Her Sādhaka by means of Sattva-pradhāna rajoguṇa, [4] Who is pictured as wearing a garland of severed heads,

Because She is Śabdabrahman (Śabdabrahmarūpiṇī) and the heads are the fifty letters,

Whose upper and lower right hands are seen to be making the Abhaya and Vara Mudrās,

Because She both destroys the dangers, and grants the desires of Sakāma-Sādhakās, Whose upper left hand is depicted as wielding a sword,

Because She severs the bonds of illusion for the Niṣkāma-Sādhaka, Whose lower left hand is seen to hold a human head,

Because She grants him Tattvajñāna, Who is called Digambarī (space-clad)

Because being Brahman (Brahmarūpiṇī) She is free from the covering of Māyā [5] and unconcerned (Nirvikāra), [6] Who is pictured as having a waist-chain of human hands,

Because hands are the principal instrument of work (Karma) and at the close of a Kalpa all Jīvas with their Karmas are merged in the Avidyā Śakti of Mahāmāyā, Who is seen standing on the breast of corpse-like Śiva,

Because the Supreme State (Paramapada) and Svarūpāvasthā or Mahādevī (one with Śiva) is Nirguṇa and changeless (Nirvikāra), Who is seen in Viparīta-maithuna [7] with Mahākāla,

Because at the beginning of a Kalpa She who is ever blissful (Nityānandamayī), and being united with Śiva, feels pleasure in the work of creation which She effects by bringing the changeless Paraśiva under Her dominion (Vaśībhūta), Who is again said to live in the cremation ground,

Because when at the end of a Kalpa all things in the universe from Brahmā to a blade of grass are dissolved in Mahākāla, She is in and one with that Mahākāla, who may be thus compared to a cremation ground, and because at the death of Jīvas She exists as the individual (Vyaṣṭi) Jīvātmā in the burning ground, Whose Yantra for worship is composed of a circle symbolizing Māyā, an eight-petalled lotus denoting the eightfold Prakṛti, three Pentagons representing the fifteen Avayavas and a Bindu denoting Śiva-Śakti,

Because She is, as Paramātmā, in the gross and subtle bodies consisting of the three Guṇas and twenty-four Tattvas, Whose Bīja 'Krīm', [8] the Queen of Mantras is pure Sattva Guṇa, and consciousness (Caitanyamayī) and grants both Enjoyment and Liberation, Who is worshipped as Dakṣiṇā because She alone grants the full fruits of all forms of Upāsanā and Yajña.

May She, this Mahādevī, who is Saccidānandarūpiṇī and forgiveness itself, pardon all offences committed by me in the explanation of this Her Hymn.

Śaṁbhu with His five mouths is unable to relate Thy qualities. Pardon all my childishness. Be propitious. Guard my life, guard my repute and guard my wife, sons and wealth. And at death grant me Liberation.

O Mother of the World, obeisance.

ŚRĪ VIMALĀNANDA-ŚVĀMĪ

[1] See Mūṇḍakopaniṣad, 1-2-4.

[2] This is a play on the word Ghana which means mass and black or dark blue cloud. Cidghana is massive, compact, unmixed, pure Consciousness (Cit). Again She is Nirguṇa and stainless but is also Meghāṅgī (cloud-bodied) because through Adhyāsa of the three Guṇas She appears varicoloured just as a cloud in itself colourless appears white, blue, and so forth by contact with the sun's rays. So Devī-Purāṇa says, 'Just as the uniform cloud appears as of many colours, so does She too through the instrumentality of the Guṇas.'

[3] Keśa = K + A + Īśa. And K = Brahmā, A = Viṣṇu, and Īśa = Rudra. The Niruttara-Tantra says, 'Kālī who is Aniruddha-saraśvatī, is the great desire-granting tree, the sole Cause of Enjoyment and Liberation for Brahmā, Viṣṇu and Maheśa.'

[4] White Teeth stand for the white Sattva Guṇa, the red Tongue stands for the red Rajo-Guṇa and Delusion is the Tamo-Guṇa. The meaning is, the Mahāvidyā is represented with a lolling tongue because She first destroys the Sādhaka's Tamo-Guṇa by increasing his Rajo-Guṇa, and large teeth because by increasing his Sattva Guṇa and suppressing his Rajo-Guṇa She grants him the state of Nirguṇa-Brahman. In the Dhyāna of Tārā it is said, 'Ugratārā Herself destroys the *Jādya* (unconscious nature) of the three worlds by putting it in her skull-cup.'

[5] In the eighteenth century work of Kamalākānta called Sādhakaranjana it is said: 'Of the Nirākāra-Brahman, understand, Māyā to be the Ākāra' (Nirākāra-brahmer ākāra dekha Māyā). The Śūnya has no form until encircled by Māyā.

[6] Vikāra is also 'change'. She is then in Her changeless aspect.

[7] Coition in which the woman assumes the dominant role. Śakti is active and Śiva is the passive principle.

[8] The Śvāmi also points out that the 'Kr' sound in this Mantra is also to be found in the word Christ and in the Mussulman's Karīm. See Māya Tantra Ch. vii for the Yavana-Bīja.

Hymn to Kālī

(Karpūrādi-Stotra)

Verse One

O MOTHER [1] and Spouse of the Destroyer of the three cities, [2] they who thrice recite [3] Thy *Bīja* [4] formed by omitting from *Karpūra*, the middle and last consonants and the vowels, but adding Vāmākṣī and Bindu, [5] the speech of such, whether in poetry and prose, like that of men who have attained all powers, [6] issues of a surety with all ease from the hollow of their mouth, O Thou who art beauteous with beauty of a dark rain cloud. [7]

Commentary
(Inner Sense)

With respectful obeisance to the beauteous feet of Svāmī Ramānanda I write this Svarūpa-vyākyā named the Grantor of Pure Bliss (Vimalānandadāyini). [8]

'Oh Mother' (Mātah)

The root Mā = to measure, to which is added the suffix tṛch = Mātṛ: that is, She who measures out or gives: She who grants enjoyment or Liberation according as the Sādhaka is desire-ridden or free from desires.

'Spouse of the Destroyer of the three cities'

The three cities are three bodies, gross, subtle, causal. She is the Śakti of Him who grants Liberation from these bodies. As the Power-holder (Śaktimān) and His Power (Śakti) are one, it is She who is grantor of such Liberation. Kaivalya-Upaniṣad says, 'From the Ātmā, the root, the bliss, looking on all alike who abides within the three cities, is born the multiple and various world and into Him these three cities are merged.'

'They who recite'

That is meditating on the same as being one with the Ātmā of the Sādhaka. Kālikā-Śruti says, 'One should always think of Ātmā as Kālī. Those who do, attain the fourfold Puruṣārtha whether directly desired or not.' Todala-Tantra (Ch. vi) says, 'Oh Devī, K grants Dharma, R grants Kama, I grants Artha and M grants Mokṣa. Oh Beloved, the recital of these combined gives Nirvāṇa Mokṣa.'

'This (Etat)'

Thy Sattva saccidānanda aspect denoted by the Bīja 'Krīṁ'.

'Triple (Trihkritang)'

That is the triple aspect Sāttvika, Rājasika, Tāmasika.

'Bīja'

Denotes the aspect in which Thou art the Cause or the World. Although as Saccidānandarūpiṇī Thou art Nirguṇa when free of Māyā characterized by the Karma of Jīvas and Kāla, Thou becomest the seed in the creation of the world, what time Jīvas must enjoy the fruit of their Karma. In the Devīgītā, Devī says 'Then I who am Ātmā, Cit, Parabrahman and called the "One" assume the Bīja (seed) aspect through union with My own Śakti. The causal body of which I have aforetime spoken is Avyakta in which the world exists as seed (Bīja) from which issues the subtle body.'

'Karpūram'

Saguṇa-Brahman the Kalpaka or fashioner of the World.

'Omitting therefrom'

Omitting from Mūlaprakṛti composed of Sattva, Rajas, and Tamas Guṇas the middle Rajas Guṇa which is Ū and the last Tamas Guṇa which is M. It is thus composed of Sattvaguṇa alone. The Jñānasaṁkalinī-Tantra says, 'A is Sāttvika, U is Rājasa, M is Tāmasa. Prakṛti is these three.'

'Adding'

Powerful to give Nirvāṇa Mokṣa and by Māyā to grant the desires of Sādhakas; and in whom the pure Sattvaguṇa predominates. The Tantra Kalpadruma says, 'K on account of its brilliance is the Citkalā, Jñāna. 'Associated with the fiery letter (R) She is auspicious and full of all Tejas. As "I" She grants the desires of Sādhakas. As Bindu She grants Kaivalya.'

'Beauty of dark clouds'

Thou who should be meditated upon as of a dark (Nīla) colour because Thou art Cidākāśa and dost possess the compact Tejas Śuddhasattvaguṇa. In the Nirvāna Prakaraṇa of Yogavāśiṣṭa it is said, 'Because Śivā is Vyoma She is seen as black.' Tripurāsārasamuccaya says, 'As being Liberation, She who is attained by devotion (Bhakti) should be meditated on as being like the sky itself free from clouds.'

[1] The Divine Mother of the World in Her aspect as *Dakṣiṇa-kālikā* that is the beneficent Grantor of *Nirvāṇa*.
The Kālikāhṛdaya says: 'I worship *Kālī* the Destructress of *Kāla* the Shining One, who is the *Bīja Krīm* who is *Kāma* who is beyond *Kāla* and who is *Dakṣinakālikā*.' Gandharva-Tantra says: 'Hrīm, I bow to *Mahādevī* who is *Turīya* and *Brahman*. He who remembers Her does not sink in the ocean of existence.' *Candī* says: 'Oh Thou whose Body is pure Plana who hast three divine eyes, who weareth the crescent moon, to Thee I bow for the attainment of all good.' (V)

[2] *Śakti* of Maheśa who destroyed the *Asura* named *Tripura* (*Tri* = three; *Pura* = city) along with his three cities in Heaven, Earth and the Nether regions (V).

[3] Recite (*Japanti*); utter repeatedly with mind fixed on the meaning of the *Mantra* (V). Lit, 'make *Japa*.' The word 'recite' is employed as the nearest English equivalent, but is not accurate, in so far as in *mānasa Japa* the action is purely mental, and in *Japa* of the next lower degree (Upāṁśu) there is movement of the lips only, but no utterance.

[4] The 'seed' *mantra*. *Bīja* is seed, the cause of the *Mantra* body (V). According to the Nityā-Tantra, *Mantras* are of four kinds—*Pinda, Kartarī, Bīja* and *Mālā* according to the number of syllables, See as to *Bīja*, A. Avalon's 'Garland of Letterś.

[5] That is, *Karpūraṁ*, less the vowels *a, ū, a*, and the consonants *pa* and *ra m* = *Kṛ* + *Vāmākshī* ('the left eye' or long vowel *ī*), with the Nādabindu superimposed = *Krīṁ* which accomplishes all desire (Tantrasāra), is *Mantrarāja* (Śyāmārahasya-Tantra) (K.B.). Tantrarāja says, 'letter *Ka* is Thy form.'

[6] *Siddhi*, or success. *Siddhi* is that which is sought for (*Sādhya*) and is the result of *sādhana*, the training of the higher psychical and spiritual faculties. It includes the eight great powers, *Aṇimā, Laghimā*, etc., the power of motion and suspension in space, and others mentioned in the Skanda Purāṇa and other works. The Devī is Herself *Mahāsiddhi* (*Lalitāsahasranāma*, v. 55).

[7] *Dhvāntadhārādhararucirucire*. Just as dark clouds, by shedding nectar-like rain, cool the earth parched by the sun's rays, so too dost Thou, by shedding the nectar of Thy Grace, give immortality to Sādhakas tormented by the three forms of pain (*Ādhyātmika, Ādhibhautika, Ādhidaivika*). The *Rudrayāmala* says, '*Devī* is Supreme *Śakti* and delivers from all difficulties. She is dark with the refulgence of a million suns and is cooling like a million moons.' (V).

[8] Vimalānanda is also the name of the Commentator.

Verse Two

O MAHEŚI, [1] even should one of poor mind [2] at any time recite but once another doubled *Bīja* of Thine, composed of *Īśāna*, [3] and *Vāmaśravaṇa*, [4] and *Bindu;* [5] then, O Thou who hast great and formidable ear-rings of arrow form, [6] who bearest on Thy head the crescent moon, such an one becomes all powerful, [7] having conquered even the Lord of Speech [8] and the Wealth-Giver, [9] and charmed countless youthful women with lotus-like eyes. [10]

Commentary

'Maheśi'

Possessor of the great Power of creating, preserving and withdrawing.

'At any time' (Kadācit)

Durgārāma-Siddhāntavāgīśa is of opinion that by the use of Kadāchit it is meant that unlike other religious Karma which can be done only in a state of purity (Śuci), Japa of the Mantra of Kālī can be done at any time whether one is in a state of purity or not (Śaucāśauca-kāla). Here he says one should not give up the worship if there be a birth or death in the house. The Tantra-Śāstra says that one should do Japa of the Mantra, whether one is in the state of purity or not, and whether walking, standing or sleeping.

'Recite' (Japati)

Meditate upon.

'Of dual aspect' (Dvandvam)

Having the dual aspect of Śiva-Śakti. The Tantra-Śāstra speaks of the King of Mantras being generated by the union of Śiva and Śakti

'Another Bīja' (Bījamanyat)

Thy causal (Kāraṇa) aspect which is the Bīja Hūṁ. In the Yāmala it is said, 'It is with the double Śabdabīja (which is Hūṁ) that She awakens the mass of Śabda.'

'Īśāna'

Is Īśvara. Kathopaniṣad says, 'Puruṣa is the size of only a thumb. He is like smokeless fire, the Ishāna of what has been and will be. He is to-day and He is to-morrow. This is That.' Indu is immortality. Vāmaśravaṇa is the power of granting speech and of attracting forms (Rūpa). The Tantrābhidāna says, 'Ū is Bhairava, subtle, Sarasvatī . . . attractor of forms.'

Who dost grant Nirvāṇa liberation. The Mahānirvāṇa-Tantra says, 'The forehead of Her who is Nityā, Kālarūpā, Arūpā, and Śiva Himself is marked with the moon on account of immortality.'

'Dost bear the half-moon' (Chandrārddhacūde) 'Earrings'

Whose earrings (things very dear) are formed of two Sādhakas who are like Maheśvara and simple as boys; that is child-like simple Sādhakas who have true knowledge are dear to Her. In the Vivekacūdāmaṇi it is said, 'Just as a boy plays with toys heedless of hunger and other pain so the wise man plays happy, unattached and selfless.' Such a Sādhaka attains all forms of knowledge and riches and can charm the whole world.

(Mahāghorabālāvataṁse)

There is however another reading given by Durgārāma-Siddhāntavāgīśa namely Mahāghorābalāvataṁse, that is whose earrings are formed of frightful arrows (Bāna).

[1] *Śakti* or *Maheśa* the Lord of even Brahmā, Viṣṇu and Rudra (V). The Devī as Īśvarī, (Ruler), of the Universe and Spouse of Nirguṇa Maheśvara. Īśvara, according to the Liṅga-Purāṇa, when associated with *Tamas*, is Rudra the Destroyer; with *Rajas*, the One born from the golden egg, Brahmā; and with *Sattva*, Viṣṇu.

[2] *Mandacetāh* who is not capable of devotion to thy lotus feet according to Commentator K.B.; for, as the Brahmāṇda-Purāṇa says, all sin is expiated by remembrance of the feet of the Supreme Śakti.

[3] That is, *Ha*.

[4] The 'left ear,' or long vowel *ū*.

[5] *Nāda-bindu*—that is, *H + ū + ṁ = Hūṁ Hūṁ*. He who makes Japa of *Hūṁ* is more praiseworthy than Deva or Asura (Viśvasāra-Tantra) (K.B.)

[6] Worn by Kālī: reading Bāna instead of Bāla as to which see *post*.

[7] Viśvasāra (K.B.).

[8] *Bṛhaspati*, *Guru* of the *Devas*.

[9] *Dhanada*, i.e. *Kubera*, Lord of Wealth, King of the Yakṣas; according to one account the son, and, according to another, the grandson of Pulastya (see Muir, OṢ., T. iv, 481, 488; v, 483; i, 492).

[10] That is, to them are given eloquence and learning, riches and beauty.

Verse Three

O KĀLIKĀ, O auspicious Kālikā [1] with dishevelled hair, [2] from the corners of whose mouth two streams of blood trickle, [3] they who recite another doubled *Bīja* of Thine composed of *Īśa*, [4] *Vaiśvānara*, [5] *Vāmanetra*, [6] and the lustrous Bindu, [7] destroy all their enemies, and bring under their subjection the three worlds. [8]

Commentary

'Kālikā'

Ka is Brahmā, A is Ananta, La is Ātmā of the universe, I is subtle, Ka is Brahmā, A is Ananta. (Tantrābhidāna). Thus it is said that Mahādevī is the subtle, beginningless and endless Ātmā of the universe. 'Thou who art Brahman without beginning or end.' In the Asitāstotra in the Adbhutarāmāyaṇa Śrī Rama says, 'I bow to that Thine aspect which is Puruṣa without beginning and end, the unmanifest Kūtastha superior (to Thine aspect) as Prakṛti, the Ātmā of the universe appearing in multiple and differing forms.'

[Durgārāma-Siddhāntavāgīśa derives the word Kālikā as follows:—He who dissolves (Kalayati) the world is (Kāla or Śiva). And She who shines (Dīvyati) that is plays (Krīdati) with Him is Kālika Kāla + ikan + ā = Kālikā.]

'With dishevelled hair' (Vigalitacikure)

That is one who is free from all Vikāras such as the passion for arranging the hair and so forth.

'Streams of blood' (Asradhūrā)

This blood indicates (the red) Rajas Guṇa. Mahādevī is without that for She is Śuddha-sattva-guṇa.

'Recite' (Japati)

Meditate upon.

Of dual aspect (Dvandvaṁ)

The Bījā Hrīṁ is both Śiva and Śakti. In the Devīgītā Mahādevī says, 'H is the gross body, R is the subtle body, I is the causal body. I am Hrīṁ the Turīya.'

'Īśa'

Who is the aspect of subtle Bīja.

'Vaiśvānara'

Which is full of Tejas.

'Vāmanetra'

That is, with Māyā consisting of pure Sattva-Guṇa.

'Indu'

This is, the Śakti which gives immortality.

'Three syllabled Dakṣiṇā'

Dakṣiṇe is Dakṣinā in the vocative, and the latter is the Saccidānanda aspect which grants Kaivalya and is indicated, by the three-syllabled Mantra. Nirvāṇa-Tantra says, 'The Sun's son (Death) is established in the south (Dakṣiṇa). The name of Kālī makes him flee in all directions with fear. Hence She is called Dakṣiṇa in three worlds.' Kāmākhyā-Tantra says, 'Just as guerdon (Dakṣīṇa) given at the end of rite, causes it to be fruitful and gives Liberation, so this Devī grants the fruit of all Karma and hence She is called Dakṣiṇa-Kālī.' The same Tantra also says, 'Puruṣa is on the right (Dakṣiṇa) and Śakti on the left. The left conquers the right and becomes the grantor of great Liberation. Hence She is called Dakṣiṇakālī in the three worlds.'

[Durgārāma construes these words as follows: Dakṣiṇe tryakṣare ati (by Saṁdhi tryakṣare'ti) that is Dakṣiṇe ati tryakṣare. As Upasargas can shift their position 'ati' has been placed in the verse after Tryakshare. Atitryakshare is the vocative of Atitryakṣarā. Atitryakṣarā means Atikrāntah (Adhahkṛtah or placed under) Tryakṣarah (Śiva) yayā (by whom) She: that is, She who has placed Śiva under Her. The whole then means 'Oh Dakshiṇa who dost stand on Śiva.' Tryakṣara literally means the three lettered one which is the Praṇava (Oṁ) and is used for Śiva. The Mahiṁnastotra (see 'Greatness of Śiva' Ed. A. Avalon) calls Śiva 'Oṁ' and another Stotra calls Him Tryakṣaramaya.

The same commentator then says that there is a different reading for Dakshiṇe tryakṣareti, namely, Dakshiṇe Kāliketi which he explains in two ways (*a*) Dakshiṇe Kālike'ti = Dakshiṇe Kālike ati = Dakshiṇe atikālike. The last word is the vocative of Atikālikā which means Atikrāntā (Sadṛśīkritā, made similar to) Kālikā (Meghajālaṁ; a bank of cloud) yayā (by whom) She—that is, She who looks like a bank of cloud; the whole then meaning 'Oh Dakshiṇā who hast the appearance of a bank of clouds' (*b*) Dakṣiṇe Kāliketi = Dakṣine Kālike iti which means Oh Dakṣiṇā Kālikā. The word 'iti' is Svarūpārthaka that is simply indicates that She is addressed as Dakṣiṇā Kālikā. Examples of the elision of 'I' after 'E' in Saṁdhi are Śakuntaleti and Meghajāle'pi Kāliketi.]

[1] The Devī. See Mahānirvāṇa-Tantra, chap. xiii and chap. iv, verse 31: 'At the dissolution of things it is Kāla who will devour all, and by reason of this He is called Mahākāla; and since Thou devourest Mahākāla Himself, it is Thou who art the supreme primordial Kālikā'.
Kālikā is *Brahmarūpiṇī* (V).
[2] *Vigalitacikure*, as is the worshipped *nāyikā*. See *post*.
[3] *Sṛkkadvandvāsradhārādvayadharavadane*. Kālī is so represented as having devoured the flesh of the demons. The Mahānirvāṇa-Tantra, chap. xiii, verse 9, says: 'As She devours all existence, as She chews all things existing with Her fierce teeth, therefore, a mass of blood is imagined to be the apparel of the Queen of the *Devas*.' Esoterically blood is Rajas Guṇa.
[4] That is, *Ha*, as to which see Kāmadhenu-Tantra, chap. ii; and Prānatoṣinī, 53 *et seq*.

[5] Lord of Fire, whose *Bīja* is *Ra*.
[6] 'Left eye,' or fourth vowel long *ī*.
[7] *Nāda-bindu*; the Bīja is thus *H* + *r* + *ī* + *m* = *Hrīṁ Hrīṁ*. In Svatantra-Tantra *Ha* (*Vyoma*) is said to denote manifestation; *Ra* (*Vahni*) is involution; and Ī maintenance of the worlds.
[8] The earth, upper and nether worlds (see Viśvasāra-Tantra and Phetkāriṇī-Tantra). *Tribhuvanaṁ*, that is *Devas, Men, Nāgas* and so forth in-habiting *Svarga* (Heaven), *Martya* (Earth) and *Pātāla* (Nether world) (V).

Verse Four

O DESTRUCTRESS of the sins of the three worlds, auspicious [1] Kālikā, who in Thy upper lotus-like left hand holdest a sword. [2] and in the lower left hand a severed head; [3] who with Thy upper right hand maketh the gesture which dispels fear, [4] and with Thy lower right hand that which grants boons; they, O Mother with gaping mouth, [5] who reciting Thy name, meditate in this way [6] upon the greatness of Thy mantra, possess the eight great powers [7] of the Three-Eyed One [8] in the palm of their hands. [9]

Commentary

'Sword' (Kṛpāṇam)

The sword is knowledge (Jñāna) by which the bonds of ignorance of the desire-free Sādhaka are severed. See Śivadharmottara.

'Severed head' (Chinna-muṇḍaṁ)

The human head is the seat of Tattvajñāṇa free of attachment.

'Terrible countenance' (Prakatita-radane)

Her white teeth indicative of the white self-manifesting Sattva-Guṇa bite the red lolling tongue indicative of Rajas Guṇa and suppress both Rajas and Tamas by Sattva.

'Precious Mantrās' (Manu-vi-bhavaṁ)

The three 'Krīṁ' Bījas represent the Cidghana aspect of Devī, the two Hūm Bījas the Sattva-Guṇa aspect and the two 'Hrīm' Bījas the Rajah-pradhāna-sattva-Guṇa aspect.

[Durgārāma-Siddhāntavāgīśa explains this in the following different ways: (*a*) Manuvibhava = the Vibhava or Saṁpatti (precious possession) of Manus or Mantras. This precious possession is the name in the vocative case 'Dakshiṇe Kālike.' The meaning of the passage then is that those who recite Thy name Dakshiṇe Kālike, which is the precious possession of Mantras, and meditate on this Thine appearance possess the Powers and so forth. (*b*) Manuvibhava is the Vibhava of the Manu that is the twenty-two syllabled Mantra of Kālī. This possession is the name Dakshiṇā Kālikā. (*c*) Manuvibhava = Manu (Mantra) vibhava (Ghataka) of which (the Devī's body) is the body of which Mantra is the generator. The bodies of the Devatās are produced by their Mantras. The passage thus means that, they who recite Thy name Dakshiṇā Kālikā and meditate on this Thine appearance generated by Mantra possess the virtues mentioned above.]

See last Verse.

Kālikā (Kālike)

'Three eyed one (Tryaṁbaka)'

[The same commentator (Durgārāma) offers three explanations of the term Tryaṁbaka used for Śiva (*a*) He who has three Aṁbakas or eyes is

Tryaṁbaka, (*b*) He who has three Mothers or Aṁbās is Tryaṁbaka. The Kālikāpurāṇa says, 'As Hara is born of three Mothers He is known, even amongst Devas, by the title Tryaṁbaka.' (*c*) Todala-Tantra says 'the Vidyā Bhuvaneśvarī is in Heaven, Earth, and the Nether world (Pātāla). He who delights in the Devī as threefold in three places is called Tryaṁbaka. He is with Śakti and is worshipped in all Tantras.']

[1] *Dakshiṇā*, the beneficent grantor of *Nirvāṇa*. (V)
[2] *Khadga*, the peculiar heavy sword with the blade curved at the tip so named, used to behead the sacrificial animals.
[3] The Devī is the destroyer of the wicked.
[4] The Devī is the dispeller of all fear, and makes with Her hand the *mudrā*. The right upper hand makes the gesture of dispelling fear, or the gesture of assurance of safety (*Abhayamudrā*) and the right lower hand makes the gesture of granting boons (*Varamudrā*). (V) The *Sādhaka* seeks fearlessness, which is the great gift of the Goddess, who is *Bhayāpahā*, 'remover of fear.' 'If thou art remembered in times of difficulty, Thou takest away all fear' (Mārkaṇḍeya-Purāṇa). At the same time it is she who fills the ignorant with terror (Paśuloka-bhayaṁkarī) that is, those devoid of the knowledge of non-duality, for 'fear comes when there is duality' (Br. Up. 1-4-2, Lalitā, v. 99).
[5] *Prakatita-vadane* (see '*Daśa-Mahāvidyā Upāsanārahasya*,' by Prasanna-Kumāra-Śāstrī). *Vimalānanda* reads *Prakatitaradane*, that is, with big protruding teeth. The *Yoginī-Tantra* says, 'Supreme eternal, large-toothed, smeared with blood.' The *Tārākalpa* speaks of '*Syāmā* of the colour of a new (freshly formed) cloud, with large breasts, terrible with protruding teeth.' (V)
[6] As stated—that is, *Krīṁ Krīṁ Krīṁ Hūṁ Hūṁ Hrīṁ Hrīṁ* which with *Dakṣiṇe* makes ten syllables.
[7] *Siddhi*—that is, *Aṇimā, Laghimā, Garimā, Prāpti, Prākāṁya, Iśitva, Vaśitva, Kāmāvasāyitā* the power of becoming small, great, heavy, light, etc., which are inherent in Īśvara, and are attainable by Yogis who become Īśvara and gain *Āiśvarya*. By realization of the self, that Divine state which is the universal Self is manifested, as also the eightfold manifestation of the Divine power.
[8] *Tryaṁbaka* or *Śiva*. According to Tarkālaṁkāra's Commentary on Mahānirvāṇa-Tantra, *Tryaṁbaka* means the father of the three Devas, Brahmā, Viṣṇu, and Rudra. The *Ṛgvidhāna* uses it as an equivalent of Mahādeva. The Mahānirvāṇa-Tantra says: 'As She surveys the entire universe, which is the product of time, with Her three eyes—the Moon, Sun, and Fire—therefore She is endowed with three eyes' (*Ullāsa* xiii, verse 8) The Moon, Sun, and Fire are the *Icchā, Kriyā, Jñāna* and other *Śaktis* (see the Ṣat-cakranirūpaṅa of Pūrnānaṇda-Śvāmī) and Serpent Power by A. Avalon.
[9] 'By him who carries a flower its odour is enjoyed without seeking. By him who looks upon himself as the universal Self the powers (of Brahmā, etc.) are enjoyed' (Commentary of Sureśvarācārya on tenth Sloka of *Dakṣināmūrti Stotra*).

Verse Five

O MOTHER, they who recite Thy charming *Bīja*, composed of the first of the group of letters, [1] followed by *Vahni*, [2] *Rati*, [3] and beautified by *Vidhu*, [4] thrice, the *Kürca Bīja* [5] twice, and thereafter, O Smiling Face, the *Lajjā* [6] *Bīja* twice, followed by the two *Thas*, [7] they, O Spouse of the Destroyer of the Deva of Desire [8] contemplating Thy true form, [9] become themselves the Deva of Love whose eyes are as beautiful as the petals of the lotus which Lakṣmī holds in Her playful dance. [10]

Commentary

'Whoever' (Ye, ye)

Even the most sinful. The Kālīkularahasya says, 'Whoever he be who remembers Durgā with or without reverence is delivered from evil and attains the supreme end.'

'Recite' (Japanti)

Meditate upon.

'Thy Bīja'

[Durgārāma Siddhāntavāgīśa calls it the nine syllabled Bīja.]

First letter (Vargādyaṁ)

The aspect of Consciousness (Cinmayarūpa) which is the beginning of creation.

Placed on Vahni (Vahnisaṁsthaṁ)

Full of Tejas.

'Associated' (Vidhu-rati-lalitaṁ)

That is cooling and beautiful.

'Thrice' (Trayaṁ)

'That is the three aspects of Sattva, Rajas, Tamas.

'Kürca'

Is Śabdabrahman.

'Lajjā'

Is Brahman associated with Māyā.

'Two Thas'

Svāhā the revealing Śakti of Fire.

'Smiling face' (Smitamukhi)

Because She is always blissful.

'Spouse of the Destroyer' (Smara-hara-mahile)

Śakti of Śiva who is the Destroyer of passionate Desire; that is She destroys the lust, anger and so forth of Her Sādhakas.

'Thy true form' (Śvarūpaṁ)

That which is not different (in essence) from Jīvātmā. Śvarūpa is explained here as the Rūpa of Śva, that is Ātmā, meaning the Oneness of Paramātmā and Jīvātmā. Kālikā-Śruti says, 'One should always think of Ātmā as Kālī'. Kālīkulasarvasva says, 'He who worships the spouse of Śiva thinking that his Ātmā is Kālikā's Ātmā and meditating on the Śiva-like Guru is Sadāśiva Himself.' Yoginī-Tantra says, 'He who thinks, even if it were for a moment, "I am Brahman" to him the Devī gives unending fruit. One's own body should always be thought of as the body of the Iṣṭadevatā. And so the whole world should be considered as Her body.'

[Durgārāma explains Svarūpa in the following ways: (*a*) The true form is that indicated in the previous or following verses. (*b*) It is that of the nine-syllabled Mantra. (*c*) It is that indicated by the letters composing the Mantra. For instance Varadā-Tantra says that in 'Krīṁ', K is Kālī, R is Brahmā, I is Mahāmāyā, Nāda is the Matrix of the universe and Bindu is the Dispeller of Sorrow. In 'Hūṁ', H is Śiva, Ū is Bhairava, Nāda means the Supreme and Bindu is the Dispeller of Sorrow. In Hrīṁ, H is Śiva, R is Prakṛti, I is Mahāmāyā, Nāda the Generatrix by the Universe and Bindu the dispeller of pain. Contemplation on Mantras constituted of these letters reveals their Caitanya. Japa of Mantra without knowing its Caitanya is useless.]

'Become themselves' (Kāmarūpā bhavanti)

They acquire the power of assuming whatever form they desire and of charming the whole world with their beauty.

[1] That is, *Ka.*

[2] Deva of Fire, or *Ra.*

[3] Śakti of Kama, God of love, or long Ī.

[4] The moon, or *Nāda-bindu.* The Bīja is, therefore, *K + r + ī + ṁ = Krīṁ.*

[5] That is, *Hūṁ.*

[6] *Hrīṁ*, literal meaning of *Lajjā*, is modesty.

[7] Or Svāhā, Śakti of Agni. The *mantra* is, then, *Krīṁ, Krīṁ, Krīṁ, Hūṁ, Hūṁ, Hūṁ, Hrīṁ Svāhā*, or the nine-lettered *Vidyā*, or feminine *mantra*, which ends with *Svāhā* (see Viśvasāra-Tantra).

[8] *Smarahara* or *Siva*, who destroyed Manmatha with fire from his central eye of wisdom when the latter sought to distract him by passion from his *Yoga*. The Devī, according to the Brahmavaivarta-Purāṇa, restored Manmatha to life (see as to this Bhāskararāya's Commentary on the Lalitā, verse 34).

[9] *Svarūpaṁ*, that is true form as described in the first and other verses (V).

[10] *Lakṣmī* is associated with, holds, and stands on the lotus, hence Her titles—Kamalā, Padmā, *Padmālayā, Padmadhārini* (see Lakṣmīstotra in Tantrasāra, p. 577, Rasik Mohan Chatterjee's edition).

Verse Six

O DEVĪ [1] of full breasts, [2] whose throat is adorned with a garland of heads, They who meditating [3] recite any one or two or three of Thy very secret and excelling *Bījas* or all thereof [4] together with Thy name, [5] in the moonlike face of all such the Devī of Speech [6] ever Wanders, and in their lotus-like eyes Kamalā [7] ever plays. [8]

Commentary

'Devī'

The self-manifest one.

'Full breasts' (*Pīnastanādhyā*)

The milk of these is the, food with which She nourishes the world and the drink of immortality with which She liberates Her Sādhakas.

'Whose neck' (Muṇda-sragatiśaya-lasat-kaṇṭi)

She who is Śabdabrahman consisting of 50 Letters. Niruttara-Tantra says, 'She is adorned with a garland of heads representing the 50 letters.' Kāmadhenu-Tantra says, 'In My throat is the wonderful Bīja of 50 letters.' Again ' I worship the Mother the source of the universe, Śabdabrahman itself, blissful.' Viśvasāra says, 'Blissful Brahman is adorned with Śabdabrahman and within the body is represented by all Mantraś.

'Bīja'

Mūrti (appearance) in the individual aspect as Prājña, Taijasa, and Viśva and in the aggregate as Īśa, Sūtra and Virād. Devīgītā says 'the causal self is Prājña, the subtle bodied one is Taijasa and the gross bodied one is Viśva.' Similarly Īśa is spoken of as Īśa, Sūtra and Virād. The first is the individual (Vyaṣti) aspect and the second the aggregate (Samaṣti) aspect.

Eyes (Netra)

Not to speak of themselves being wealthy, the sight of them gives wealth to others. Bhairava Tantra says that Kamalā and the Devī of speech never forsake them for three generations downwards.

[1] *Devī* which comes from the root *Div* to shine, is the Shining One (V).

[2] *Pināstanādhye* (see also Bhairavīstotra in Tantra-sāra, p. 596). The physical characteristics of the Devī in swelling breasts and hips are emblematic of Her great Motherhood, for She is *Śrīmātā*. See also as to the former, Durgā-*Dhyāna* in Devī-Purāṇa, which speaks of her large and rising breasts (*Pīnonnata-payodharāṁ*); the Annapūrṇā-*Stava* (*Vakṣojakuṁbhāntarī*); Bhuvaneśvarī-*Stotra* (*Āpivara-stanatatīṁ*); and the Saraswatī-*Dhyāna* (*Kucabharanamitāṁgīṁ*). The Annapūrnā-*Dhyāna* (*Annapradāna-niratāṁ stanabhāra-*

naṁrāṁ) speaks of Her limbs as weighted by Her breasts. The Mahābhāgavata describes Her as naked, terrific, with fiery eyes, full and erect breasts, and dishevelled hair; and the Lalitā (verse 15) says: 'Her golden girdle supports Her waist, which bends under the burden of Her breasts, thrice folding the skin below Her bosom' (*Stanabhāra-dalanmadhya-pattabhandha-valitrayā*).

[3] *Bhāvayantah*, that is, meditating on the naked, full-breasted, black form with dishevelled hair as stated in Her *Dhyāna*, and which is the *Artha* of the particular *Mantra*. The *Bhūtaśuddhi-Tantra* says, 'A Mantra should be recited mentally meditating the while on the form of the *Devī* denoted by it ' (V).

[4] Any one of the aforesaid Bījas or the whole that is, the whole nine-lettered *Vidyā* in full. Which according to the Kumārī-Tantra cited in Tantraratna is *Krīṁ, Krīṁ, Krīṁ, Hūṁ, Hūṁ, Hūṁ, Hrīṁ, Hrīṁ, Hrīṁ*. Śyāmārahaśya quoting Kālikā-Śruti, says that the whole *Vidyā* should be recited once, twice or thrice, or the whole *mantra* with '*Dakṣiṇe Kālike* between the Bījas.' (K. B.) Thus, *Krīṁ, Krīṁ, Krīṁ, Hūṁ, Hūṁ, Hrīṁ, Hrīṁ, Dakṣiṇe Kālike, Krīṁ, Krīṁ, Krīṁ, Hūṁ, Hūṁ, Hrīṁ, Hrīṁ*.

[5] *Dakṣiṇe Kālikā*.

[6] *Sarasvati*. The Bhāradvāja-Smṛtī says Sarasvatī is She who ever resides in the tongue of all beings, and who causes speech.

[7] *Lakṣmi*: for them is all learning, wealth, and prosperity (see Mahānirvāṇa-Tantra, *Ullāsa*, vii, verse 50).

[8] In the other words they become rich and learned.

Verse Seven

O MOTHER, even a dullard becomes a poet who meditates upon Thee raimented with space, [1] three-eyed [2] Creatrix [3] of the three worlds, whose waist [4] is beautiful with a girdle made of numbers of dead men's arms, and who on the breast of a corpse, [5] as Thy couch in the cremation-ground, [6] enjoyest Mahākāla. [7]

Commentary

'Dullard' (Jadacetāh)

One whose mind is smitten with passion for the world.

'Poet' (Kavīh)

A great Jñānī.

'Meditates' (Dhyāyan)

Who in mental vision sees Thee who art Saccidānandarūpiṇī.

'Whose loins' (Bāhuprakarakṛta-kāñcīparilasannitaṁbām)

At the end of each Kalpa all Jīvas abandon their gross bodies, and existing in their subtle bodies in which their respective Karmas inhere, form part of the Avidyā which is in the causal body of the Brahmarūpiṇī associated with Her own Gūṇās (Svaguṇa) until they are liberated at some future time after the commencement of the next Kalpa. Hence the girdle adorning the loins, lower belly and generative organ of the Mahādevī virādrūpiṇī, capable of producing children is fashioned of the arms and hands of dead Jīvas. For these arms and hands were their principal instruments for the doing of work (Karma). The Śāktānandataraṅgiṇī says, 'With Karma is a Jīva born, with Karma he dies, and in the next body again that Karma is attached to him.' Devīgītā says, 'In Her at dissolution Jīvas and their Karmas are merged in undifferentiated mass, just as all which is done (Vyavahārā) merges in dreamless sleep (Suṣupti).' Again the Devī says, 'It is I who create the whole world and enter therein with Prāṇa, Māyā, Karma and so forth.'

'Raimented with space' (Digvastrām)

Raiment is the covering of Māyā. She is without that and above Māyā.

'Three-eyed' (Triṇayanām)

Having knowledge of the three divisions of Time, past, present and future.

'Creatrix' (Vidhātrī)

She who at the beginning of the next Kalpa gives birth and enjoyment to Jīvas according to their respective Saṁcita Karma.

'On the breast of a corpse' (Śavahṛīdi)

The corpse is Nirguṇa-Brahman. The couch is the support (Ādhāra). On Nirguṇa-Brahman as Thy Ādhāra. that is established in Thine own state (Pada) as Nirguṇa-Brahman. Gāyatrī-Tantra says, 'By the word corpse is indicated Brahman as the dead body (Preta).' Gandharva-Tantra says Sadāśiva is the couch on which lies the subtle Tripurasundarī.

'In the cremation ground' (Śmaśānasthā)

The cremation ground (Śmaśāna) is the great Ether (Mahākāśa) in which all creatures are merged as corpses in the Great dissolution (Mahāpralaya). In dissolution even the greatest of creatures are but corpses and hence it is a cremation ground.

'Dost enjoy Mahāhāla' (Mahāhāla-surata-prayuktām)

At the end of a Kalpa, there being no creation, She being inactive, and there being nought but supreme Brahman, She being in-separate from Paraśiva, experiences Herself as unlimited (Akhaṇda) Bliss.

[1] The Devī is naked, as is Śiva, for, like Him, She is clothed with space, and is the great void itself (Mahāśūnya).

[2] *Triṇayanāṁ*. The Three eyes are Sun, Moon and Fire (V). *Mahānirvāṇa-Tantra* says, 'Three eyes are attributed to *Kālikā* because She observes the whole world with such eyes as the Sun, the Moon, and so forth'. See as to the meaning of these three terms which do not merely denote these luminaries and elements, A. Avalon's 'Serpent Power' and Studies in *Mantra-Śāstra*'.

[3] *Vidhātrim*, who provides Enjoyment and Liberation for all Jivas. (V).

[4] *Nitaṁba*, literally, buttocks but the girdle goes all round. Kālī is represented as so girdled.

[5] The corpse (*Śava*) represents *Śiva* (V) because He is inactive whilst his *Śakti* it is who does everything. *Śavahṛdi*—that is, on the breast of Śiva (*Viparītarati*). The Devī is given the dominant position in her union with Her consort, because She is *Kartri* (actress), and He is *Bhoktā* (unacting enjoyer). According to Sāṁkhya, *Puruṣa* is neither producer nor produced, but passive, and a looker-on upon the actions of *Prakṛti*. It is not the *Puruṣa* who is active in the creation of the world, but it is She who, in the light of His gaze, dances the world-dance. So Kubjikā-Tantra says: 'Not Brahmā, but Brahmānī, creates; it is Vaiṣnavī, not Vishnu, who protects; Rudrānī, not Rudra, who takes all things back. Their husbands are like dead bodies.' For in respect of power they are dependent on their Śakti. As to the *Sādhana*, see Prāṇatoṣinī 622, *Viparitaratau japtvā nirvāṇapadavīṁ vrajet*. Two corpses are sometimes pictured, the lower being the eternally quiescent Śiva, and the upper being the Śiva united with Śakti in creation. Similarly the Devī is represented as reclining on a couch made of five corpses, which are the Mahāpreta (see Bhairavayāmala, Lalitā verse 174, etc). The *Mahāpretas*, whose *Bīja* is *Hsau*, are Sadāśiva, Īśāna, Rudra, Viṣṇu, and Brahmā.

[6] The site of certain forms of Tantrik *Sādhana*, such as *Śavāsana Muṇdāsana*, etc., as to which the Phetkāriṇī-Tantra says that it is an excellent place for *Sādhana*. He who makes japa a number of times on a corpse in a cremation-ground attains all manner of success (*Siddhi*).'

[7] Parama-Śiva.

Verse Eight

THOSE who truly [1] meditate on Thee, the Spouse of Hara, [2] who art seated in [3] the cremation-ground strewn with funeral pyres, corpses, skulls, and bones, and haunted by female jackals howling fearfully; who art very youthful, [4] and art in full enjoyment upon [5] Thy Spouse, are revered by all and in all places. [6]

Commentary

'Meditate on' (Dhyāyanti)

That is see with unperturbed mind.

'Spouse of Hara' (Haravadhūṁ)

Hara is He who removes (Harati) the threefold pains (Ādhyātmika, Ādhibhautika, Ādhidaivika) of Jivas. His spouse is Śakti, that is She who grants Liberation to Jīvas and is Saccidānandarūpiṇī.'

'Hast entered' (Praviṣṭāṁ)

Art established.

'Flaming' pyre (Prakatitacitāyāṁ)

Cit-śakti On account of Her being self-manifested. Caṇḍī speaks of 'Her who pervades the whole universe as consciousness (Cit).'

'Fearful' (Ghorābhih)

That is very powerful.

'Jackals' (Śivābhih)

That is Mahābhūtas which are auspicious (Śiva) before being made fivefold (Pañcīkṛta).

'Skulls and bones' (Muṇḍāsthi-nikaraih)

The white colour of the skulls and bones indicates the white Sattva-guṇa. Hence associated with the Sattva and other Guṇas of the Jīvas dissolved in Mahāpralaya.

'Ever youthful' (Atiyuvatīṁ)

That is She is always the same, fresh, unchanging, and un-wasting.

'Satisfied with enjoyment ' (Santushtām-uparisuratena)

She, after subduing Parama Śiva to Her will, has willingly enjoyment in the work of creation, preservation and dissolution. Nirvāṇa-Tantra says, 'The Vāmā (She who is on the left) is the Grantrix of Great Liberation after conquering the Dakṣiṇa (Śiva who is on the right).' Gandharva-Tantra says, 'She who is the Sun, Moon, and Fire and half of Ha (Śiva) puts down the Puruṣa and enjoys him from above.' Niruttara-Tantra says, 'When Nirguṇā Kālī becomes Saguṇā She is engaged in Viparītarati.' The Yoga-vāṣiṣtha in the Nirvāṇa-Prakaraṇa says, 'Natural unity is Śiva. Creation is (compared with it) unnatural.' That is the Mahādevī is Nirguṇa-Brahman in Her Svarūpa aspect and the subversion of this Svarūpa is the cause of creation.

'Nowhere' (Kvacidapi na)

In no birth.

'Humiliated' (Paribhavah)

That is they are not subjected to birth, death, and rebirth and attain Nirvāṇa.

[1] Commentator K. B.: where *param* is said to mean 'rightly,' or meditation alone without *japa*.
[2] *Śiva*.
[3] *Praviṣtām*, 'literally Entered '.
[4] *Atiyuvatim*. She is without childhood or old age. The *Sāradātilaka* says, 'Although Thou art primordial, Thy youth is ever fresh'. (V)
[5] *Santuṣṭāṁ uparisuratena*, that is *viparītarati*, or *viparītavihāra* as to which see note 5 of last *śloka*.
[6] Commentator K. B.: literally 'They nowhere suffer (*Kvacidapi na*), that is, neither in this nor the next world defeat or humiliation.'

Verse Nine

WHAT, indeed, O Mother, [1] can we of so dull a mind say of Thee whose True Being [2] not even Dhātā, [3] Īśa, [4] or Hari [5] know? Yet, despite our dullness and ignorance, our devotion towards Thee makes us talk of Thee. [6] Therefore, O Dark Devī, [7] forgive this our folly. Anger towards ignorant creatures such as we, is not befitting Thee. [8]

Commentary

'Mother'

Of us all including Brahmā, Viṣṇu, and Rudra. In the Devi-Sūkta, Viṣṇu says, 'One, subtle, and unchanged, and yet many, Thou dost give birth to millions of worlds. Who am I Viṣṇu, and who is the other Śiva and who are the Devas that we and they should be able to (fully) sing Thy praises? ' In the Mārkaṇdeya-Purāṇa, Brahmā says, 'When Viṣṇu, Īśvara and myself owe our appearance to Thee who has the power to (fitly) praise Thee?' In Viṣṇuyāmala, Viṣṇu says to Devī 'Oh Mother, none know Thy supreme aspect. The heavenly ones therefore worship that gross (Sthūla) aspect of Thine in the form of Kālī and the rest.' The Mahākāla-saṁhitā says, 'When Dhātā was not, nor Viṣṇu, nor Kāla, when the five Bhūtas were not, then Thou the Cause wert alone as the Supreme Brahman, the Being of all that is.'

(Asite) 'Unlimited'

She is not limited by the Guṇas and is Nirguṇā.

[1] *Jānāmi;* origin of the three worlds.
[2] *Paramaṁ*, or 'reality' (Commentator K. B).
[3] *Dhātā* is *Brahmā* who dispenses the fruits of *Karma*. (V)
[4] *Śiva. Īśa*: *Rudra* who wields the power of *Īśvara-hood*. (V)
[5] *Hari*: *Viṣnu* who dispels the threefold sorrows of *Jīvas*. (V)
[6] *Tathāpi tvadbhaktir mukharayati. Tathāpi*: still, despite our dullness and ignorance (V) *Tvadbhaktih*: inclination to sing Thy praises (V). *Mukharayati*: impels to utter words in praise of Thee (V)
[7] This is literal but According to V *Asite* = unlimited one. Mahākala-saṁhitā says, 'Unthinkable, unlimited, *Śakti* Itself, which is That on which all that is manifested rests, beyond the *Guṇas*, free of the opposites (*Dvandva*) to be apprehended only through *Buddhi*: Thyself alone art Supreme Brahman.' (V)
[8] As one does not become angry with animals (Paśu or animal and ignorant men also called Paśu) because they do wrong, so do not be angry with us. It is moreover, the part of the great to overlook the faults of their inferiors (Commentator. K. B.)

Verse Ten

IF by night, [1] Thy devotee [2] unclothed, with dishevelled hair, recites whilst meditating on Thee, [3] Thy *mantra*, [4] when with his *Śakti* [5] youthful, full-breasted, and heavy-hipped, such an one makes all powers subject to him, and dwells on the earth ever [6] a seer. [7]

Commentary

'Laya Yoga'

Is here described in this and following verses. Gheraṇda-Saṁhitā says, 'One should become Śaktimaya by doing Yoni Mudra. One should be in Paramātmā with sweet Śṛngārarasa (love sentiment) and being Blissful (Ānandamaya) should unite with Brahman.' The Gorakṣa-Saṁhitā says, 'Raising the Śakti with the Jīva to the Lotus in the head one should become Śaktimaya and uniting with Śiva should think of all forms of happiness and enjoyment.' The Tantra-Kalpadruma says, 'One should meditate on Devī Kuṇdalinī as Iṣtadevatā, ever youthful, of the age of sixteen, full-breasted, dark, subtle, appearing as creation and in the form of creation, maintenance and dissolution (Ṣṛṣti-sthiti-layātmikā).'

'Thy devotee' (Bkaktah)

Here the Divya Sādhaka who is a Yogin.

'By night (Naktam)'

That is, awaking in Brahmavidyā which (though Light) is darkness for all ordinary creatures. The Bhagavadgītā says, 'The self-controlled man awakes in what is night to all creatures.'

'Naked' (Vivāsāh)

That is, stripped of the covering of Māyā: that is awakened.

'Dishevelled hair' (Galitacikurah)

That is, with mind free from all restlessness. The word Cikura means both hair and restless.

'Meditating' (Dhyāyan)

On Thee as in enjoyment of Sāmarasya bliss with Paramaśiva.

'Enjoying' (Ratāsaktām)

By doing Laya of (merging) the Jīvātmā in Kuṇdaliṇī-Śakti, the ever-youthful, all-pervading Genetrix and Preserver of all Jīvas. The creative and nourishing function of Kuṇdaliṇī is indicated by the epithets 'heavy-hipped' and 'full-breasted.'

[1] *Naktaṁ*. At dead of night. The Phetkāriṇī-Tantra says, 'By night, naked with dishevelled hair in union with *Śakti*, by him is all *Siddhi* gained'. The Kālikrama says, 'The *Paśu* devoted to his own *Ācāra* should recite his *Mantra* a lakh of times by day. The *Vira* or *Divya* should recite it a lakh of times by night.' Kubjikā-Tantra says 'Such as are in *Paśubhāva* are but *Paśus*. They should not touch a rosary nor recite *Mantra* by night.' (V)

[2] *Bhaktah*. Here a *Vira-Sādhaka*. Niruttara-Tantra says, 'The *Mantrin* who has received *Ābhiṣeka* should do *Kulapūjā*. Oh Devī the *Mantra* of *Kāli* does not become *Siddha* without *Kulācāra*.' (V)

[3] *Tvāṁ dhyāyan*. Mentally seeing Thee in his heart as ever in the Enjoyment of union with *Mahākāla*. (V)

[4] Thy *Mantra* is the aforesaid great *Mantra*. (V)

[5] He is *Ratāsakta*, the meaning of which is as follows: *Sa mantraṁ japati yadā sa śobhanāṅgapratyaṅgaśālinyā manohāriṇyāyuvatyā śaktyā saha maithunāsakto bhavati*. Whilst in union (*Maithuna*) the mind must be concentrated on *Devī Kāli* and *japā* must be done of Her *Mahāmantra*. The devotee should not think of aught else.

[6] So also Phetkāriṇī-Tantra (ch. x) says:

'*Rātrau nagnah śyānas ca maithune ca vyavasthitah. Athavā muktakeśash ca tena syuh sarvvasiddhayah. Staṁbhanaṁ mohana-caiva vaśīkaraṇaṁ eva ca*.'

Here *Athavā* means if the *Sādhaka* is without a *Śakti*; then recitation of *mantra* with dishevelled hair gives the same *siddhi*.

[7] *Kavi* which has not here the limited sense of 'Poet.'

Verse Eleven

O SPOUSE of Hara, [1] should (a *Sādhaka*) daily [2] recite Thy *mantra* for the space of a year meditating the while [3] with knowledge of its meaning [4] upon Thee intent [5] upon Thy union [6] with the great Mahākāla, above whom Thou art, [7] then such a knower [8] has every pleasure that he wills upon the earth, [9] and holds all great powers [10] in the grasp of his lotus-like hands.

Commentary

'Spouse of Hara' (Haravadhū)

Charmer of Mahākāla.

'Mentally recite' (Vicintya japati)

The Kaulāvalī says that mental (Mānasā) Japa is a hundred times more efficacious than verbal (Vācika) Japa.

According to Durgārāma the words may also mean 'recite' keeping in mind the Artha or meaning and so forth of the Mantra. For it is said that he who does not know the Artha of Mantra, the Caitanya of Mantra, and Yoni-mudrā is without success (Siddhi) even if he do Japa of the Mantra a million times.

'Unperturbed mind' (Susthībhūya)

The Kulārṇava-Tantra thus enjoins: 'Beloved when doing Japa of a Mantra one should be calm, pure, sparing in food, reverential, self-controlled, unaffected by the opposites (Dvandva), steady of mind, silent and self-disciplined.

'Meditating on Thee' (Vicintyatvām)

The Kaulāvalī-Tantra says, 'One should meditate upon the Spouse of Śiva before Japa and after meditation should again do Japa.' The Sādhaka who does Japa and meditation together soon attains success.

'Upon Him' (Vipāritām)

(The original is 'Viparītah' in the first case and Durgārāma therefore makes it an adjective of the Sādhaka who he says unites with his Śakti in Viparīta Maithuna. Vimalānanda however reads it as Vipāritām in the second case making it an adjective of 'Thee' (the Devī) who is the object of meditation,)

'Great Powers' (Mahāsiddhinivahāh)

Such as that by which is gained Sālokya, Sārūpya, Sāyujya and Nirvāṇa forms of Liberation.

[1] *Śiva.*

[2] *Sadā*: Means 'always' here 'daily' (K.B.)

[3] *Vicintya*, that is, who has mentally thought of the letters of the *Bija* and their meaning, which is mental *japa* (*Mānasa japa*), defined in Narasiṁha-Purāṇa (cited in the Āhnikācāra-tattva of Raghunandana) as the repetition in the mind, letter by letter, syllable by syllable, of the mantra, meditating at the same time upon its meaning.
[4] That is upon *Varṇa-saṁsthāna* or placing of the letters and their meaning and so forth.
[5] *Susthibhūya*—that is, whose senses are not directed to any other object (Commentary, K.B.)
[6] *Atiśayamahākālasuratām.*
[7] *Vipāritām* (see sloka 7, note 5.)
[8] *Vidvān* whose sole aim is *Mokṣa.*
[9] Literally 'wandering freely on Earth' (Commentary, K.B.)
[10] *Siddhi* (see *ante.*)

Verse Twelve

O MOTHER, Thou givest birth to and protectest the world, and at the time of dissolution dost withdraw to Thyself [1] the earth and all things; therefore Thou art Brahmā, and the Lord of the three worlds, the Spouse of Śrī, [2] and Maheśa, [3] and all other beings and things. [4] Ah Me! how, then, shall I praise Thy greatness?

Commentary

'Dost withdraw' (Saṁharati)

That is dost make the world lose itself in Thy Causal (Kāraṇa) body.

'Dhātā'

She is the creative Śakti of Brahmā.

'Husband of Śrī' (Śrīpatih)

She is the preservative Śakti of Viśṇu whose spouse is Śrī or Lakṣmī.

'Maheśa'

She is the dissolving Śakti of Rudra.

'All things' (Samastaṁ)

Thou art both the material and instrumental cause of the world. The Triputā-Stotra says, 'Thou art Earth, Brahmā, and Creatrix of the world. Thou art also Water, Viṣṇu, and Preserver of the world. And thou art Fire, Rudra and the Dissolver of the world. As the Air of the world thou art Aiśvarya.' Another Stotra says, 'She assumes three forms of body for the purpose of creation, maintenance and dissolution. The world being constituted of the three Guṇas, Brahmā, Viṣṇu and Rudra are Her Vikṛtis.'

[1] It is commonly said that She destroys but not so. Devatā does not destroy (*Na devo nāśakah*). Man does. She takes back what She has put forth.
[2] *Viṣṇu*, husband of *Lakṣmi*.
[3] *Śiva*. The *Trimūrti* is, in fact, Her manifestation.
[4] *Prāyah sakalaṁ api*, that is, all moving and unmoving things (Commentary, K.B.). For the Devī is *Viśvarūpiṇī* in the form of the whole universe. She is the objective world, '*jadātmikā*' (Lalitā, verse 90), as well as its Cause.

Verse Thirteen

O MOTHER, people there are who worship many other *Devas* than Thyself. [1] They are greatly ignorant, and know nothing of the high truth, [2] (but I) of my own uncontrollable [3] desire for Thee approach Thee, the Primordial Power, [4] who dost deeply enjoy the great Bliss arising from union (with Śiva), [5] and who art worshipped by Hari, Hara, Viriñci, and all other Devas. [6]

Commentary

'Deluded' (Vimūdhāh)

That is, devoid of discrimination.

'Enlightened' (Vibudhaih)

The Bagalā-Stotra says, 'Oh four-armed, four-headed, worshipful Parameśvari, Oh Devi Aṁbikā who art ever worshipped with devotion by Kṛṣṇa, Oh Parameśvari who art worshipped by the Lord of the daughter of Himālaya, grant beauty, Grant victory' and so forth.

'Ādyā'

Who art before and the beginning of the world.

'Union' (Rati)

Which is Viparīta as above described.

'Wine'

That is Rasa.

[1] That is, thinking that other *Devas* grant greater boons (Commentary, K.B.). Cf. also what Śaṁkarācārya says about the worship of other Devas in fourth śloka of the *Devyaparādha-kṣamāpana-stotra*, and see *Devibhāgavata* (V. 19) (Hymn to Jagadaṁbikā).

[2] *Paramam*, that is, *Tattvaṁ*.

[3] For he is a devotee (Bhakta) whose desire for Her is so great that he cannot control but is controlled by it.

[4] *Ādyā*.

[5] *Rati-rasa-mahānanda-niratām*. The Devī delights in creation, which is the fruit of Her union with the *Puruṣa* (Śiva). 'Great Bliss,' for, as on the physical plane yadrūpaṁ paramānandam tan nāsti bhuvanatraye (Mātṛkābheda-Tantra, chap. ii), it is the counterpart on that plane of the ecstatic union which produced the Universe itself. It is the reflection of the higher Bliss attainable even here by the union of Śivaśakti (in the form of Kuṇdalinī) in the *Sahasrāra*. Some read *Rasikāṁ* for *Niratāṁ*.

[6] *Viṣṇu*, *Śiva*, and *Brahmā*. What, then, is the use of praying to *Brahmā*, *Viṣṇu*, and *Śiva* when they themselves worship Her? (Commentary, K.B.). Cf. also Devibhāgavata, *loc. cit.* The *Devi* is Mother of all, from *Brahmā* to the lowliest worm (*Ābrahmākhilajanani*, Lalitā 67).

Verse Fourteen

O KĀLĪ, spouse of Giriśa, [1] Thou art Earth, Water, Fire, Air and Ether. [2] Thou art all. Thou art one and beneficent. [3] What can be said in praise of Thee, O Mother? Of Thy mercy show Thy favour towards me, helpless as I am. By Thy grace may I never be reborn. [4]

Commentary

'Kālī'

Dispeller of the fear Kāla or Death.

'Thou art Earth' (Dharitrī kīlālangshachirapi samīropi gaganam)

Guptārṇava-Tantra says, 'Thou art Earth, Thou art Water, Thou art Fire, Thou art the Air of the world, Thou art Ether, Thou art Mind as Manas, Ahaṁkāra, Mahat (Buddhi) and Thou art Prakṛti. Thou art also, Oh Mother, Ātmā. Thou art the Supreme. Nothing is greater than Thee. Oh Devī of terrible form showing Thy teeth may my sins be forgiven me.' The Triputā-Stotra also says, 'Thou art the Ādhāra-Śakti and the Ādhāra. Thou dost pervade the world and the world is in Thee.'

'One' (Ekā)

Without a second.

'Beneficent' (Kalyānī)

Because She grants Nirvāṇa Liberation to Jīvas.

'Spouse of Girisha' (Giriśaramanī)

Spouse of Śiva. Or He who is in the Giri or Kūta is Giriśa that is Kūtastha-Brahman; His spouse or Śakti. Though changeless (Nirvikārā) Thou dost appear as the twenty-four Tattvas, namely, Earth and the rest through Thy Māyā. The Devīsūkta of the Ṛg-Veda says, 'Thou who art one and many, subtle and the Vikāras (gross things) and giveth birth to millions of universes.'

'All' (Sakalaṁ)

Śruti says, 'Verily all this is Brahman'.

'Helpless' (Agatikaṁ)

On account of liability to rebirth despite Sādhana.

[1] The Lord who inhabits the mountain, whereas, *Giriśa* is Lord thereof.
[2] Liṅgapurāṇa says, Devī becomes matter' (*Kṣetra*). She is *Kṣetrasvarūpā*, that is, the field or matter which is known by the soul (*Kṣetrajña*). See Lalitā Sahasranāma (fourth hundred) for the Brahman who creates the visible world Itself enters into it (*Tat sṛṣtvā tād evānuprāviśat.*)
[3] *Kalyāṇi*. According to the Padma-Purāṇa, Devī is worshipped as *Kalyāṇi* in the Malaya Mountain.

[4] *Bhavaṁ anu na bhūyān mama januh,* that is, liberated. The Śyāmārahasya reads *Bhavaṁ ananubhūyāt,* using *bhavaṁ* as meaning *duhkhaṁ* (pain), arising from *bhava* (the world) (K. B.).

Verse Fifteen

HE, O Mahākālī, [1] who in the cremation-ground, naked, and with disheveled hair, intently [2] meditates upon Thee [3] and recites Thy *mantra*, and with each recitation makes offering to Thee of a thousand *Ākaṇda* flowers [4] with seed, [5] becomes without any effort a Lord of the earth. [6]

Commentary

'And' (Tu)

For Divya Sādhakas.

'Mahākālī'

Or Parabrahmarūpiṇī.

Cremation-ground' (Śmaśānasthah)

The cremation-ground is Parabrahman into which in the great Dissolution (Mahāpralaya) all beings go as though corpses. 'In the cremation ground' therefore, means devoted to Parabrahman.

'Naked' (Dikpatadharah)

That is, free from the covering of Māyā; whose Consciousness is untainted.

'Meditates on Thee' (Dhyānaniratah)

That is, upon Thy Saccidānanda aspect. The Rudrayāmala says, 'He who follows the Kula path should do Japa of Mantra seeking protection from Devī who is Consciousness, Bliss and Source of knowledge, who is all Tattvas whose refulgence is that of millions of flashes of lightning.'

'Sunflowers' (Arkānāṃ)

Flowers of feeling such as compassion, forgiveness and so forth which are functions of the Mind called the Sun in the Brahmarandhra. The Jñānasaṁkalinī-Tantra says, 'Oh Beloved, the mind is seated on the surface of the sun and life on that of the moon.' The Yājñavalkya-Saṁhitā says, 'The Moon is known to be in the Idā and the sun in the Piṅgalā (Nādī).

'Self-produced Bīja' (Nijagalitavīryena)

This Bīja is here the nectar which naturally flows from the thousand-petalled Lotus. The Mahānirvāṇa-Tantra says, 'The Heart-Lotus should be offered for seat, the nectar (Amṛta) shed from the Sahasrāra for water to wash the feet, the mind as the offering (Arghya), Memory (Citta) is offered by way of flowers, and the vital airs (Praṇa) as and by way of incense.' Jñānasaṁkalinī-Tantra says, 'Libation (Tarpana) to the Supreme Liberatrix should be made from out the vessel of the Moon and Arghya should be given from out the vessel of the Sun. Compassion, wisdom, and forgiveness are flowers as is also control of the senses. So too are charity (Dayā) and religious merit. Non-injury (Ahiṁsā) to any being is an excellent flower. Bliss is a flower and so too is the worship of the Sādhaka. Whoever offers these ten flowers attains to the feet of the Liberatrix.' In this verse Savikalpasamādhiyoga is indicated.

[1] *Mahākālī, Śakti* of *Mahākāla.*
[2] *Susthah*: with undistracted mind. (V)
[3] *Tava dhyāna-niratah,* that is, Upon Thy form. (V)
[4] *Arka* = Sun flowers known as *Ākaṇda* (V) not the flower so called in English.
[5] *Nija-galita-vīryeṇa kusumaṁ.* Thus the offering is not only of the flowers of the *Ākaṇda* plant, *yatah sādhakah devyai sva-vīrya-miśri-tārkapuṣpāni samarpayati.* Durgārāma-Siddhāntavāgīśa cites the Mahākālasaṁhitā as saying that the *sūryapuṣpa* should be offered in the same way with *japa* of the *mūlamantra (svavīryamiśrita-sūryapuṣpāni).* The *vīrya* does not, refer to the sap of the plant. *Nija* refers to the *sādhaka.* 'Along with, that is dipped in or that is spread over with.' *Mahākāla-samhitā* says, A *Kaula-Sādhaka* in the cremation-ground, naked, dishevelled and with tranquil mind, should offer a thousand sunflowers with seed reciting the while his *Mantra.* After meditating and worshipping with great devotion he should recite the Hymn' (V).
[6] That is, a king or *rājā.* So the Phetkāriṇī-Tantra says that wealth, strength, eloquence, intelligence, and the love of women (*Sarvayoṣitpriyah*) is gained.

Verse Sixteen

O KĀLĪ, [1] whoever [2] on Tuesday at midnight, [3] having uttered Thy *mantra*, makes offering even but once with devotion to Thee of a hair of his *Śakti* [4] in the cremation-ground, [5] becomes a great poet, a Lord of the earth, and ever goes mounted upon an elephant. [6]

Commentary

'Kālī'

Dispeller of the fear of Kāla or Death.

'Whoever'

Here a Divya Sādhaka.

'Midday' (Madhyāhne)

At noon.

'Devotion' (Premnā)

That is Parabhakti.

'Offers' (Vitarati)

Merges in Thee, that is, attains Nirvikalpa-Samādhi. Pātanjala-Sūtra says that Nirvikalpa-Samādhi is attained by suppression of the Vṛtti of mind.

'In the cremation-ground' (Citāyām)

In thee as Consciousness (Cit).

'Bīja'

That is here nectar which issues on the enjoyment of the union of Kula-kundalinī and Paramaśiva. The Gandharvamālikā-Tantra says, 'Oh beloved One, the Queen of Devas unites with Paraśiva and in a moment, Oh Devī Parameśvari, nectar is forthwith produced. That nectar, Oh Devī, is like the juice of lac. With it, Oh, Mistress of the Devas, libation (Tarpaṇa) should be offered to the supreme Devatā.'

'At home' (Gṛhe)

In the thousand petalled Lotus (Sahasrāra).

'Hair with its root' (Cikuraṁ samūlaṁ)

The mind with its functions. It is such Sādhaka who gains both enjoyment and Liberation.

[1] *Kālī* is destroyer of *Kāla* (V).

[2] 'Whoever' is here a *Vīra Sādhaka*.

[3] *Madhyāhne*. Noon or (here) midnight, *Kakārakūtarahasya* says, 'Whoever naked and with dishevelled hair, on a Tuesday, at midnight, does *Homa* in the cremation-ground with hair, nails, seed and whatever adheres to the *Sammārjañī* and offers them after having uttered the *Mūlamantra* and recited Thy name a thousand times attracts to him the Lord of the Earth' (V).

[4] The offering is stated in the words *grihe sammārjanyā parigalitabījam hi chikurang samūlang madhyānhe vitarati chitayāng kujadine*. These words have received various interpretations, of which the two chief alternatives are given. *Gṛhe* is by some translated as 'at home,' in distinction from the cremation-ground to which, according to this rendering, the *sādhaka* subsequently goes to make his offering. This, however, is said to be erroneous, as the *sādhanā* takes place not in the house but in the cremation-ground. Others (see Calcutta edition) translate it as the equivalent of *grihinī*, or wife. *Sammārjanī* is by them read to mean 'comb.' *Parigalita* is translated 'removed,' in the sense that the curling of the hair of the wife is 'removed' or straightened with the comb. *Bijam* given either its primary meaning, or as the equivalent of *vīrya* is said to mean *kautilyam*, or curl of the hair. *Cikuram* is hair,' and *samūlam* qualifies it, meaning pulled out, taken off at the root. The meaning is, then, an offering is made of the wife's hair, the curls (*kautilyam*) of which have been straightened out with the comb (*sammārjanyā*), and some of which has come off at the root (*samūlam*). The correct rendering, however, is according to K. B. *Śaktisādhakayoh gṛhe maithunasamaye yonilimgasamgharṣavaśāt śaktiyonipatitaṁ vīryaliptaṁ loma devyai samarpitaṁ bhavati*. *Gṛhe* thus does not mean 'at home,' but *manmathagrihe*. The hair is from the same. *Saṁmārjanī = Śiśna*. *Samūlaṁ* qualifies *cikuram* in the sense of 'come off at the root' under the circumstances stated. *Parigalita* is 'dropped'—referring to the *vīrya*.

According to *Vimalānanda*, *Gṛhe parigalita-vīryaṁ*, is that produced by union with the *Sādhaka's svaśakti* or wife (V).

Of the words *Gṛhe saṁmārjanyā parigalita-viryaṁ cikuram samūlaṁ* the Commentator Durgārāma Siddāntavāgiśa gives the two following alternative expressions: (*a*) *Sammārjanyā* means with a comb with which the hair is put in order. P*arigalitavīryam chikuram* means hair of which the *Vīrya* or crookedness has been removed. *Gṛhe* means in the wife: for it is said the wife is the home. The whole phrase then means Wife's hair, root and all, combed out straight with a comb or (b) *Sammārjanyā Parigalita-viryaṁ* means *Śukra* produced by *Sammārjanī* here meaning *Liṅga* of the *Sādhaka*; *gṛhe* means in the abode of *Kāma* that is *Yoni* of *Śakti* together with hair, root and all.

The English translation is somewhat abbreviated with the object of giving only so much as all renderings are agreed upon. But in practice *Vīrya* is used by most in its literal sense, this is the gross meaning. The inner sense is given in the *Svarūpa-vyākhyā* which follows.

[5] According to some, the offering is made on the built-up pyre, and, according to others, on the fire after the body has been consumed. *Citā*, however, is really used as a synonym for the burning ground (*Smaśāna*). The Niruttara-Tantra (Ch. I) speaks of two Kinds of *Smaśāna*:

Śmaśānaṁ dvividhaṁ deva citā yonih prakīṛtitaṁ.

[6] That is, he becomes a *Rājā*, and has no longer to go on foot like common folk.

Verse Seventeen

THE devotee [1] who, having placed before himself, [2] and meditated and again meditated [3] upon, the abode, [4] strewn with flowers, [5] of the Deva with the bow of flowers, [6] recites [7] Thy *Mantra*, Ah! [8] he becomes on earth the Lord of Gandharvas, [9] and the ocean of the nectar of the flow of poesy, [10] and is after death in Thy supreme abode. [11]

Commentary

'Devotee' (Bhaktah)

The Sādhaka who is a Yogi on the Divya path.

'The Abode' (Kusuṁadhanusho mandiram)

The triangular Yoni Mandala in the Mūlādhāra. Nirvāṇa-Tantra says, 'In the triangle, the abode of Kāma, the Liṅga is Maheśvara.'

'With its own flowers'

Adorned with the Svayaṁbhu-liṅga which is compared to a flower. Gorakṣa-Samhitā says, 'He is truly wise who knows the supreme Tejas in the Yoni called Svayaṁbhu-liṅga. Others are but beasts of burden.'

'Lord of Gandharvas' (Gandharva-śreṇīpatih)

A great singer. It is said 'there is nothing better than a song,'

'Poesy' (Kavitvāmṛta-nadi-nadinah)

He becomes like the great poet Kālidāsa.

'Is great' (Prabhavati)

He attains Nirvāṇa on being united with Thee who are Saccidānandarūpā. Kūrma-Purāṇa says, Brahmavādīs have learnt in all Vedas and Vedāntas the one, omnipresent, subtle (Kūtastha), immovable, absolute, endless, undecaying Brahman, the sole supreme Niṣkala-Tattva higher than the highest, eternal, auspicious, wondrous.' Devīgītā says 'Oh Mountain, he in whom Parabhakti is thus generated becomes merged in Pure Consciousness.'

[1] *Bhaktah*: here the *Vira Sādhaka* (V).
[2] *Purah*: that is with the *Mandala* of *Kāma* before him (V).
[3] That is, with intensity. *Dhyāyan dhyāyan*, repeatedly meditating (V).
[4] *Kusuma-dhanuṣo mandiraṁ*. The Deva with the bow of flowers is Kama whose abode is the *Madanāgāra*. *Tantrakalpadruma* says, 'He who recites the Mantra ten thousand times meditating on the flower-covered Yoni (*Svapuṣpairākīrṇam*) of *Śakti*, of a certainty charms all with his poesy.' *Svapuṣpa* is called *Svayaṁbhukusuma* in *Tantra-śāstra*, *Mātṛkābheda-Tantra* says, 'Oh Lady of *Maheśa Svapuṣpa*, which charms all is the *Ṛtu* which first appears in a married girl (V).

[5] *Svapuṣpairākīrṇam*. The word *svapuṣpa* = *svayambhupuṣpa*—mentioned in the Tantras. The word *puṣpa* has here, and in ordinary parlance, a figurative sense, as in English. For *puspaśabdena atra ṛtur ucyate, mātṛkābheda-tantra-pramāṇānusāreṇa anūḍhāyāh kanyāyāh prathama eva ṛtur atra ucyate. Tantrāntare tu vivāhitāyā eva bālāyā ṛtur atra vivakṣitah*. The *Śyāmārahasya* reads '*supuṣpa*,' which literally means pleasing fragrant flower, but which is possibly a misprint for *svapushpa*. The meaning of the passage is as follows: *Sādhakah svasya purobhāge śaktiṁ saṁsthāpya tasyā ṛturudhirasiktāṁ yoniṁ avalokayan san devmantraṁ japati*.
[6] That is, *Kāma*, the Deva of Desire, whose bow and arrows are made of flowers.
[7] *Japati*. Recites ten thousand times (V).
[8] *Aho*. 'Ah' an exclamation of wonder (V).
[9] Celestial spirits (*devayoni*), who play and sing at the banquets of the Devas. According to the Viṣṇu-Purāṇa, sons of Brahmā 'born imbibing melody.' The *Sādhaka* thus becomes a master of dance, music and song, *Gandarva-śreṇīpatih*. He becomes a great singer and a master of melody. The *Sāhasānka* says, '*Hāhā* is called a *Gandharva* and singing also makes a *Gandharva*' (V).
[10] He becomes a *Pandita* in all literature. The Kālī-Tantra, quoted in the Kālīkalpalatā, says that in strength he becomes like the wind, in wealth of gifts like Indra, and in the musical art like Tumburu (K.B.)—a *Ṛṣi*, master of music and inventor of the *tāmbur*.
[11] Paramapadalinah prabhavati, that is, he attains nirvāṇa (K.B.).
Prabhavati: becomes capable of creating and so forth on being merged with Thy Supreme Feet (V). The word literally means 'Excels.'

Verse Eighteen

HE who at night, when in union with his *Śakti*, [1] meditates with centred mind [2] on Thee, O Mother with gently smiling face, as on the breast of the corpse-like Śiva, lying on a fifteen-angled yantra [3] deeply enlisted in sweet amorous play with Mahākāla, [4] himself becomes the destroyer of the God of Love. [5]

Commentary

'Mother' (Jananī)

The Progenitrix.

'At night' (Naktaṁ)

Midnight. Brihannīla-Tantra says, 'He who is intent on meditation at midnight or early dawn surely sees the supremely blissful aspect of Devī.'

'Meditates' (Dhyāyet)

'On Thee as not different from the Sādhaka's own Ātmā, who art Cidābhāsa in his body as a Yantra.' Gandharva-Tantra says, 'He who is in Advaitabhāva, and thinks of the self as Devatā in the three forms of body thinks of Her and his Ātmā as one. He should worship the Devī as Ātmā with the articles prescribed. The Yantra which is one's own body should be considered the best of all Yantras.' Again 'He who meditates on the Nirguṇa, unattached pure Ātmā of Tripura as not being different from his own Ātmā becomes one with Her.'

'Thee' (Tvāṁ)

That is, Brahmamayī.

'Smiling face' (Smera-vadanāṁ)

Because She is ever blissful, being Bliss itself.

'On the breast' (Mahākālenoccāih)

On the breast of Śiva who is inactive like a corpse. She divides Herself into two parts like a grain of gram, namely, Śiva and Śakti by means of Māyā associated with Iccā, Kriyā, Jñāna, whilst at the same time remaining established in Her Nirguṇa-Brahman state.

'Fifteen-cornered seat' (Tripancāre pithe)

This is the Sādhaka's own body conceived as the Yantra in which Avidyā is the encompassing circle, the eight-fold Prakṛti consisting of Earth and so forth is the eight-petalled lotus, the five Jñānendriya, the five Karmendriyā, and five Prāṇa are the five Triangles and the Bindu which is Consciousness reflected in Māyā composed of pure Sattvaguṇa is the adorning Bīja. The Gandharva-Tantra says, 'The Cakramantramaya is the Devatā's Supreme Body which is Śiva-śakti.' The Bhagavadgītā says, 'Earth, Water, Fire, Air,

Ether, Manas, Buddhi, Ahaṁkāra, these Tattvas constitute my eightfold Prakṛti.' Gandharva-Tantra says, 'The subtle body composed of uncompounded (Apañcīkṛta) Bhūta and equipped with five Prāṇas, Manas, Buddhi and ten Indriya is the vehicle for Enjoyment. Unbeginning and undefinable (Anirvācyā) Avidyā is the causal Upādhi. Know Ātmā to be different from the three-fold Upādhi.'

'Deeply enlisted' (Madanarasalāvaṇyaniratāṁ)

Always united in the reverse (Viparīta) way with Paramaśiva the Saguṇabrahman. The Gandharva-Tantra says, 'When that Supreme Śakti by putting that Puruṣa down, of Her will appears as the universe then She becomes passionate. And then becoming Herself active the Devī rises upon Bhairava and enhances Her own bliss with waves of natural pleasure.'

'Himself also enjoying' (Svayam api ratānandaniratah)

Enjoying the bliss of union in Laya with Paramātmā by Yoni-mudrā and becoming Śaktimaya himself. The Gheraṇḍa-Saṁhitā says, 'He should do Yoni-mudrā and himself become Śaktimaya. He should move in Paramātmā with the good Śṛngārarasa. Becoming Ānandamaya he should be one with Brahman.'

'Destroyer of Kāma' (Smarahara)

The Advaita-sādhaka attains Kaivalya by being merged in Thee who art Paramātmā.

[1] *Svayam api ratānandaniratah,* of which the meaning is as follows: *yadā sādhakah śaktyā saha maithunakriyāsakto bhavati, tadā sa ślokokta-dhyāna-prakārānusāreṇa deviṁ dhyāyati.*

[2] *Samāsaktah,* concentrated on Thee.

[3] Kālīkalpalatā says it is a kind of *yantra* (diagram).

Tripūñcāre pīthe. The *Yantra.* The *Kāli-Tantra* says, 'First draw a triangle. Outside it put another. Next draw three triangles. In the centre draw the *Baindava-Cakra* adorned with the *Māyā Bīja.* Draw a circle outside the six-cornered figure. Next draw the eight petals attached to the outer circle and *Bhūpura.* He who knows this great *Yantra* surely attains liberation.' *Bhūpura* is the gross body composed of the five *Bhūtas* (V). It is made with five triangles superimposed.

[4] *Mahākalenoccair-madana-rasa-lāvaṇya-niratāṁ. Mahākāla* is *Paramaśiva* (V). *Madana-rasa-lāvaṇya-niratāṁ* refers to *Viparītarati* (V).

[5] *Smarahara.* The destroyer of *Kāma* is *Śiva* Himself (V).

That is, he becomes *Śiva* Himself, who destroyed *Smara* the *Deva* of Love (Kāma), with Fire from His central eye, when the latter, by the excitation of desire (towards Pārvatī), sought to detract him from his *yoga.* Or it may be translated 'excels in beauty the God of Love.'

Verse Nineteen

O DARK One, [1] wondrous and excelling in every way, [2] becomes the accomplishment, [3] of those worshippers [4] who living in this world [5] freely make offering to Thee in worship [6] of the greatly [7] satisfying flesh, together with hair and bone, [8] of cats, camels, sheep, [9] buffaloes, goats, and men. [10]

Commentary

'Oh Black one' (Asītā)

Asitā means free from bondage. Sitā means bound. Asitā is therefore 'not bound' or eternally liberated. The root *So*, means 'to bind.' Amarakośa gives the meaning of Sita as 'bound.'

'Wondrous' (Apūrvā)

Best.

'At every step' (Pratipadam)

In succession, step by step.

'All Powers' (Sarvasiddhi)

The five Siddhis which are the five forms of Liberation. The Śivagītā says, 'Sālokya, Sārūpya, Sārṣti, Sāyujya and Kaivalya. Know these to be the five forms of liberation.'

'The flesh of' (Palalaṁ)

These animals represent the Six Enemies (Ripu) or Vices which are specially characteristic of the following animals: The goat stands for Lust (Kāma) 'as lustful as a goat (Chhāga),' the buffalo, Anger (Krodha) 'as angry as a buffalo (Mahiṣa),' the cat, Greed (Lobha) 'as greedy as a cat' (Mārjāra), the sheep, Delusion (Moha), 'as stupid as a sheep' (Meṣa) the camel, Envy (Mātsarya) 'as envious as a camel' (Uṣtra), Man, Pride (Mada) 'the Pride and arrogance of man' (Nara).

The Ānandākalpa says, 'Worship should be done by making offering of lust as goat, buffalo, and so forth '. Offering is made to Thee who art Cidrūpā of lust and other vices as articles of offering (Upacāra) in worship with the object of ridding oneself of them. Bṛhannīla-Tantra says, 'In the fire of Ātmā which flames with the ghee (Havih) of Dharma and Adharma, I ever offer in Homa by the Suṣuṁnā path, with the mind as ladle, all the functions of the senses—Svāhā.'

'In worship' (Pūjāyām)

In mental worship according to the manner prescribed.

'With hair and bone' (Loma, asthi)

That is the whole without omitting any part. Such Sādhakas attain the Sālokya and other forms of liberation.

[1] Asitā: That is Kālikā v. *post.*

[2] *Pratipadam.* The Śyāmarahasya-sārasaṁgraha reads *pratidinam* (every day) (K.B.), which seems preferable, for, as K.B. says, the worship (*pūjā*) is the general daily *pūjā*, upon which daily advancement in *siddhi* would follow.

[3] *Siddhi*: success in work; accomplishment of all which is desired (V).

[4] *Sat*, that is, *sādhu* (wise, good, pious). *Satāṁ* = *Sādhakānām* (V).

[5] That is, among men.

[6] *Pūjāyāṁ api* (see note 2), *ante.*

Pūjāyāṁ: *Naimittika* or occasional worship (V). The force of the particle *api* is that the offering is not confined to special *Sādhanā* but is made in ordinary worship also. (K.B.)

[7] *Param* (K.B.).

[8] That is flesh and all.

[9] *Maiṣaṁ.* The Śyāmarahasya-sārasaṁgraha gives also *mauṣam*, of rat's flesh. The Fetkāriṇī-Tantra has both sheep and rat's flesh (K.B.).

Śyāmārahasya says, To him who makes offering of the flesh of cats, sheep, camels, and buffaloes together with bone, hair and skin *Dākṣiṇā* is ever beneficial like a Mother.'

[10] As to this human sacrifice, K. B. says that Kings alone, and not any other, are entitled to make human sacrifice, citing the Yāmala quoted in the Kālīkalpalatā (*Rājā naravaliṁ dadyān nānyopi parameśvari*). For inner sense see Svarūpa-vyākhyā *post.*

Verse Twenty

O MOTHER, he who, being a controller of his passions, [1] eats *haviṣyānnaṁ*, [2] and, being proficient in meditation on Thy feet, rightly recites [3] Thy *mantra* a hundred thousand times by day, and he who afterwards [4] naked at night, when united with his *Śakti*, [5] rightly recites Thy great *mantra* another such hundred thousand times, becomes on earth like unto the Destroyer of Smara. [6]

Commentary

'Naked' (Nagnah)

That is free from the covering of Māyā; Nirvikāra.

'Amorous play' (Nidhuvana-vinodena)

That is enjoying the bliss of union between Ātmā and Paraśakti. The Kulārṇava-Tantra says, 'That is coition (Maithuna) in which there is the bliss arising from the union of Ātmā and Paraśakti. Others are but Enjoyers of women.'

'Becomes' (Syāt)

That is, becomes liberated whilst yet living (Jīvanmukta) like Śiva.

[1] *Vashī*. The first part of this *Śloka* refers to *Paśvācāra*.

[2] That is, one who has undertaken the *Puraścaraṇavrata*, and eats the pure form of food known as *Haviṣyānnaṁ* (K.B.).

Haviṣyāśanaratah: that is after the recitation (V).

[3] Makes *japa* (see *ibid.*).

[4] *Paraṁ*: that is, when he has been *Abhiṣikta* into *Vīrācāra*.

[5] *Naktaṁ nagno nidhuvana-vinodena*, the meaning of which is *yādā sādhakah śaktyā saha maithuna-kriyāsakto bhavati, tadā sa mantraṁ japati*.

[6] *Smarahara* or *Śiva* (see note 5 to *Śloka* 18, *ante*). The Tantrakalpadruma says, 'He who eats *Haviṣyānnaṁ*, who keeping *Devī* in mind recites the *Mantra* a hundred thousand times by day and is at night united with his *Śakti* becomes the Lord of the earth.' (V).

Verse Twenty-One

O MOTHER, this Hymn of Thine is the source from whence originates Thy *mantra*. [1] It sings of Thy real self, and contains injunctions for the worship of Thy two lotus Feet. He who reads it at midnight or at time of worship [2] even his random talk [3] becomes the nectar juice of poesy.

Commentary

'Thy real self' (Svarūpākhyaṁ)

Speaks of the Dhyāna of both Thy gross and subtle aspects.

'Reads' (Paṭati)

That is recites aloud. The Viśuddheśvara-Tantra says, 'Oh Devī, the reading of a Hymn (Stotra) mentally, or the recitation of a Mantra loudly is as ineffectual as water in a broken jar.'

'Nectar of Poesy' (Prasarati kavitvāmṛtarasah)

He becomes full of the sweetness of Poesy. The Kālīkulasarvasva says, All whose difficulties and dangers are destroyed by a single reading, as it were flies in a flame. His speech flows like the Ganges full of prose and poetry.'

[1] *Manusamuddharaṇajanuh*—that is, cause of *mantroddhāra*: formation of Mantra of Devī. The *mantra* is made known, and then impressed with the life and consciousness (*caitanya*) of the *sādhaka* (*mantra-caitanya*).

[2] *Pūjā*.

[3] That is, even his meaningless delirious talk, as in fever or madness, etc. (K.13.).

Verse Twenty-Two

NUMBERS of women with large eyes, like those of the antelope, [1] impatient for his love, ever follow him. Even the King becomes subject to his control. He becomes like unto Kuvera [2] himself. An enemy fears him as if he were a prison. Living in continuous bliss [3] the devotee is liberated when yet living, and is never again reborn. [4]

Here ends the Hymn by Śrī Mahākāla, entitled *Karpūrādistotra.*

Commentary

'Liberated' (Jīvanmukta)

And on death gets Videhamukti.

'No rebirth' (Muktah pratijanuh)

He gets Nirvāṇa in Brahman. The Mahākāla-saṁhitā says, 'Whoever constantly and with devotion reads this Hymn originating from Mahākāla, is free from danger, disease and death and in the end attains Kaivalya liberation.'

Here ends the Hymn named Svarūpastotra of Śrīmatī Dakṣiṇa-Kālikā by Śrīmān Mahākāla.

Here also ends its annotation and Svarūpavyākhyā entitled Vimalānandadāyini.

Obeisance

To Kālī the spouse of Kāla, who destroys all sin and is Kāla. [5] She who is Tārā the Saviour the Supreme Brahmavidyā who is adored by the Lotus-born Deva. [6]

She who is Śrīvidyā, desirous of the welfare of Sādhakas, on the path of Liberation, to whom Hari and Hara [6] make obeisance.

May that Devī the Mother, who appears in the form of all things, bring forth benefits for all such as sing Her praises.

Colophon

Of this King of Hymns wherein Mahākāla has described the true self of Kālikā, the Karpūrādya Hymn, untainted by worldly desire, which gives bliss to Devotees, the aforesaid Annotation containing its simple interpretation, as well as the Svarūpavyākhyā (Commentary) which gives pure joy was prepared by me Vimalānanda Svāmī for the enlightenment of Sādhakas in the Saka year 1837. Mayest Thou reside in the throat of him who reads it.

OṀ, TAT SAT, OṀ

[1] *Kuraṅga*, which has beautiful large eyes.
[2] Lord of wealth.
[3] *Kelikalayā*, by the various entertaining acts (*parihāsādinā*) of which there are sixty-four. The meaning here is that there is continuous bliss.
[4] *Kelihalayā ciraṁ jivanmuktah sa bhavati ca bhakhtah pratijanuh,* The translation in the text reads *pratijanuh* to mean as K. B. says, *Janmanivritti* or cessation of birth. But *Pratijanuh* may also mean 'birth after birth.' According to this translation *jivanmukta* would not refer to the state immediately preceding Kaivalya but, as K.B. says, *Jivadavasthānubhūtadevatā-sākṣātkāra-mukha* in which case the translation will be, He living in continuous bliss obtains direct Experience of the Devatā and is reborn life after life as Her devotee. According to the translation adopted complete liberation follows and in the other case some lower though happy state.
[5] The first Kāla is Mahākāla and the second is the produced Kāla.
[6] Brahmā.
[7] Viṣṇu and Rudra.

www.ingramcontent.com/pod-product-compliance
Lightning Source LLC
Chambersburg PA
CBHW032028040426
42448CB00006B/770
* 9 7 8 1 7 8 9 8 7 1 3 9 5 *